THE ROAD TO SHILOH

Early Battles in the West

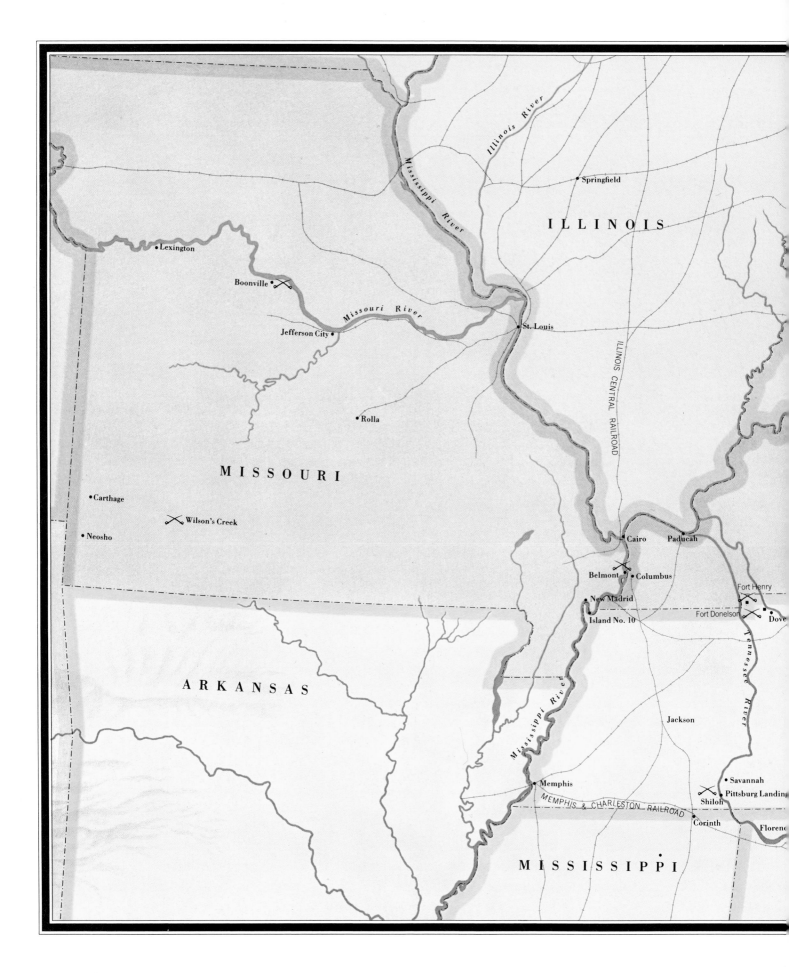

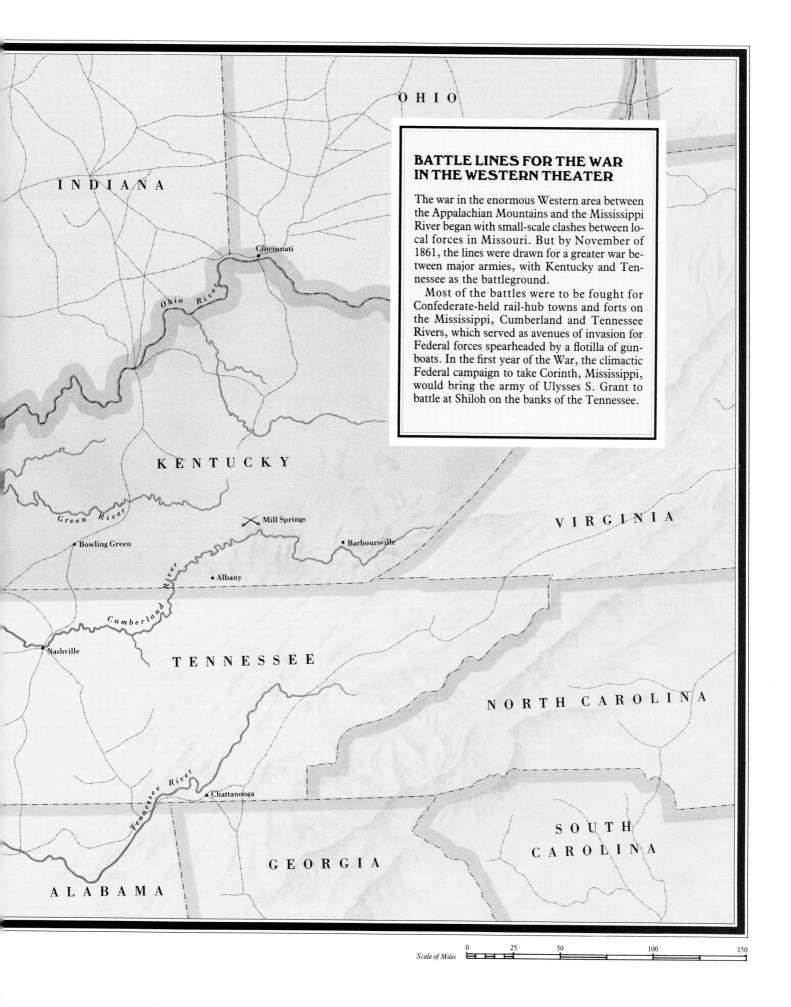

OHIO

INDIANA

Cincinnati

Ohio River

KENTUCKY

Green River

VIRGINIA

•Bowling Green

✕ Mill Springs

•Barboursville

Cumberland River

•Albany

•Nashville

TENNESSEE

NORTH CAROLINA

Tennessee River

•Chattanooga

SOUTH CAROLINA

GEORGIA

ALABAMA

BATTLE LINES FOR THE WAR IN THE WESTERN THEATER

The war in the enormous Western area between the Appalachian Mountains and the Mississippi River began with small-scale clashes between local forces in Missouri. But by November of 1861, the lines were drawn for a greater war between major armies, with Kentucky and Tennessee as the battleground.

Most of the battles were to be fought for Confederate-held rail-hub towns and forts on the Mississippi, Cumberland and Tennessee Rivers, which served as avenues of invasion for Federal forces spearheaded by a flotilla of gunboats. In the first year of the War, the climactic Federal campaign to take Corinth, Mississippi, would bring the army of Ulysses S. Grant to battle at Shiloh on the banks of the Tennessee.

Scale of Miles   0   25   50   100   150

Other Publications:

WEIGHT WATCHERS® SMART CHOICE RECIPE COLLECTION
TRUE CRIME
THE AMERICAN INDIANS
THE ART OF WOODWORKING
LOST CIVILIZATIONS
ECHOES OF GLORY
THE NEW FACE OF WAR
HOW THINGS WORK
WINGS OF WAR
CREATIVE EVERYDAY COOKING
COLLECTOR'S LIBRARY OF THE UNKNOWN
CLASSICS OF WORLD WAR II
TIME-LIFE LIBRARY OF CURIOUS AND UNUSUAL FACTS
AMERICAN COUNTRY
VOYAGE THROUGH THE UNIVERSE
THE THIRD REICH
THE TIME-LIFE GARDENER'S GUIDE
MYSTERIES OF THE UNKNOWN
TIME FRAME
FIX IT YOURSELF
FITNESS, HEALTH & NUTRITION
SUCCESSFUL PARENTING
HEALTHY HOME COOKING
UNDERSTANDING COMPUTERS
LIBRARY OF NATIONS
THE ENCHANTED WORLD
THE KODAK LIBRARY OF CREATIVE PHOTOGRAPHY
GREAT MEALS IN MINUTES
PLANET EARTH
COLLECTOR'S LIBRARY OF THE CIVIL WAR
THE EPIC OF FLIGHT
THE GOOD COOK
WORLD WAR II
HOME REPAIR AND IMPROVEMENT
THE OLD WEST

For information on and a full description of any of the
Time-Life Books series listed above, please call
1-800-621-7026 or write:
Reader Information
Time-Life Customer Service
P.O. Box C-32068
Richmond, Virginia 23261-2068

This volume is one of a series that chronicles in full
the events of the American Civil War, 1861-1865.
Other books in the series include:

The Cover: On the Shiloh battlefield, Federal
troops under Brigadier General Benjamin M. Prentiss
hold their battered line against one of a dozen
Confederate assaults on April 7, 1862. The sheer
ferocity of the two-day battle and the heavy
casualties suffered by both sides extinguished the last
hopes for a brief war with minimal bloodshed.

THE CIVIL WAR

THE ROAD TO SHILOH

BY

DAVID NEVIN

AND THE

EDITORS OF TIME-LIFE BOOKS

Early Battles in the West

TIME-LIFE BOOKS, ALEXANDRIA, VIRGINIA

The Civil War
Editor: Gerald Simons
Deputy Editor: Henry Woodhead
Designer: Herbert H. Quarmby
Chief Researcher: Philip Brandt George

Editorial Staff for *The Road to Shiloh*
Associate Editor: Jeremy Ross (pictures)
Text Editor: R. W. Murphy
Staff Writers: Adrienne George, David Johnson,
John Newton
Researchers: Feroline P. Burrage, Jayne Wise
(principals); Harris J. Andrews, Loretta Britten,
Gwen C. Mullen, Brian C. Pohanka
Assistant Designer: Cynthia T. Richardson
Copy Coordinators: Elizabeth Graham, Stephen G.
Hyslop, Anthony K. Pordes
Picture Coordinators: Eric Godwin, Donna Quaresima
Editorial Assistant: Annette T. Wilkerson

Correspondents: Elisabeth Kraemer (Bonn); Dorothy
Bacon, Margot Hapgood (London); Miriam Hsia,
Lucy T. Voulgaris (New York); Maria Vincenza Aloisi,
Josephine du Brusle (Paris); Ann Natanson (Rome).
Valuable assistance was also provided by: Lynne
Bachleda (Nashville); Carolyn Chubet (New York).

Library of Congress Cataloguing in Publication Data
Nevin, David, 1927-
  The road to Shiloh.
  (The Civil War)
  Bibliography: p.
  Includes index.
  1. United States—History—Civil War, 1861-
1865—Campaigns. 2. Southwest, Old—History—
Civil War, 1861-1865—Campaigns. I. Time-Life
Books. II. Title. III. Series.
E470.4.N48 1983   973.7'31   83-4692
ISBN 0-8094-4716-9
ISBN 0-8094-4717-7 (lib. bdg.)

The Author:
David Nevin, a writer for *Life* for 10 years, is a veteran
Time-Life Books author. He wrote two volumes in The
Epic of Flight library and four in The Old West series,
among them *The Soldiers* and *The Mexican War*. He is also
the author of *Dream West*, a historical novel based on the
career of John Charles Frémont, the noted Western explorer and Civil War general.

The Consultants:
Colonel John R. Elting, USA (Ret.), a former Associate
Professor at West Point, is the author of *Battles for Scandi-
navia* in the Time-Life Books World War II series and of
*The Battle of Bunker's Hill, The Battles of Saratoga, Mili-
tary History and Atlas of the Napoleonic Wars* and *American
Army Life*. He is also editor of the three volumes of *Military Uniforms in America, 1755-1867*, and associate editor
of *The West Point Atlas of American Wars*.

James I. Robertson Jr. is C. P. Miles Professor of History
at Virginia Tech. The recipient of the Nevins-Freeman
Award and other prizes in the field of Civil War history,
he has written or edited some 20 books, which include *The
Stonewall Brigade, Civil War Books: A Critical Bibliography* and *Civil War Sites in Virginia*.

William A. Frassanito, a Civil War historian and lecturer
specializing in photograph analysis, is the author of two
award-winning studies, *Gettysburg: A Journey in Time* and
*Antietam: The Photographic Legacy of America's Bloodiest
Day*, and a companion volume, *Grant and Lee, The Virginia Campaigns*. He has also served as chief consultant to the
photographic history series *The Image of War*.

Les Jensen, Curator of the U.S. Army Transportation
Museum at Fort Eustis, Virginia, specializes in Civil War
artifacts and is a conservator of historic flags. He is a
contributor to *The Image of War* series, a freelance writer
and consultant for numerous Civil War publications and
museums, and a member of the Company of Military Historians. He was formerly Curator of the Museum of the
Confederacy in Richmond, Virginia.

Michael McAfee specializes in military uniforms and has
been Curator of Uniforms and History at the West Point
Museum since 1970. A fellow of the Company of Military
Historians, he coedited with Colonel John Elting *Long
Endure: The Civil War Years*, and he collaborated with
Frederick Todd on *American Military Equipage, 1851-
1872*. He has written numerous articles for *Military
Images Magazine*, as well as *Artillery of the American
Revolution, 1775-1783*.

CONTENTS

The Struggle for Missouri

1

In the autumn of 1861, Brigadier General William Tecumseh Sherman was ordered west on a mission that was—he wrote his brother, Ohio Senator John Sherman—both diplomatic and military. He was to travel widely through Ohio, Indiana and Illinois, judging the morale of the population and its readiness "to oppose the Southern Confederacy." That done, he was to help recruit and train "a force adequate to the end in view."

Sherman returned from his travels both alarmed and exhilarated. He was shocked by the lack of preparedness he found, and by Washington's seeming indifference to the fate of a region he regarded as crucial. At the same time, he was excited about the strategic opportunities he sensed in the vast field of operations that lay between the Allegheny Mountains and the Mississippi. "Whatever nation gets the control of the Ohio, Mississippi, and Missouri Rivers," he wrote his brother, "will control the continent."

A fair number of shrewd men had already reached that conclusion. Chief among them was the U.S. Army's commanding general, Winfield Scott, who had advanced a grand strategy for using the Mississippi to defeat the Confederacy. As part of his so-called Anaconda Plan, Federal forces would strike south along the river, splitting the Confederacy and—in conjunction with a coastal blockade—strangling it in sections. In fact the Mississippi and its tributaries were to dictate the strategies of the war in the West and give the campaigning there

a character radically different from that of the Eastern war.

Western rivers owed their enormous importance to their great length and their direction of flow. Eastern rivers tended to flow from west to east, and were navigable only for short distances; they were less valuable as thoroughfares than as barriers to any invasion of the North or South. The big Western rivers, on the other hand, flowed from north to south, reaching into the Confederacy's heartland. These rivers were full of tricky shallows and snags, and were dangerous torrents during floods, but they more than made up for the West's lack of adequate roads and sparsity of railroads. Though attempts would be made to close the rivers with artillery batteries emplaced at strategic points, gunboats would prove that they could slip past or successfully duel with the strongest of forts. Beyond cannon's range, riverboats could put troops ashore to move against a fort by storm or by siege.

The vital core of the Western river system was the 250-mile stretch of the Mississippi between St. Louis and Memphis. Here the great river was joined by the Ohio and the Missouri. The Ohio drained all the way from the Appalachian Mountains, making it an important route for men, munitions and machinery moving from the industrial East to the Western war zone. The Ohio's two main tributaries were crucial as well. The Tennessee penetrated deep enough into Alabama to permit an invading force to flank the Alle-

Fancifully decorated, this gold sword was awarded to Confederate General Sterling Price by the city of New Orleans after his victories at Wilson's Creek and Lexington, Missouri. The sword's ivory grip takes the form of an ear of corn; its guard combines a stalk of hemp, a tobacco leaf and a cotton boll.

gheny range and attack the Confederacy from the rear; and the Cumberland hooked through Tennessee to the major industrial center of Nashville. Of slightly less wartime importance, the Missouri served as a link to states farther west, and the Illinois brought cargoes from the Great Lakes and Chicago.

Altogether, the rivers of the Mississippi system drained more than 1.2 million square miles of terrain and, being navigable over most of their lower courses, could quickly and conveniently deliver troops and supplies by boat to much of the vast central valley. Thus the fighting in the West became a far-flung war of movement as opposed to the more static war of position in the East, where the armies fought most of their battles in the 100 miles of terrain between Washington and Richmond.

The great distances involved also put an indelible stamp on the Western theater. To the despair of the generals who fought in the West, their remoteness from Washington and Richmond made for neglect; they received only such manpower and supplies as were left over after the needs of the forces in the East had been met. So they fought campaigns that were often catch-as-catch-can and sometimes helter-skelter. In turn their ability to improvise and their sheer aggressiveness earned more than a few Western generals—most notably Ulysses S. Grant and John Pope—a reputation as men who were always ready to fight.

The campaigns that moved up and down the Western rivers featured several battles that would change the course of the conflict. The first major battles would be fought for Forts Henry and Donelson—Confederate strongholds on the Tennessee and the Cumberland that protected the interior of the middle South. Then, completing the first year of operations in the West, a savage struggle would rage for two days along the Tennessee River near a Methodist meeting-house called Shiloh Church. That bloody battle would decide very little; fighting for the Mississippi Valley would continue for more than a year. But the final outcome of the war in the West would depend very largely on which side could transcend casualties as heavy as those both sides suffered for the first time in the fields and woods at Shiloh.

The Shiloh battle was thus a watershed in the nation's attitude. Nobody after Shiloh could fail to understand the War's brutality—or its terrible cost. The sacrifice here of more American lives than had been lost in all of the country's previous wars destroyed any possibility of a negotiated peace; the War henceforth could be won only by more sacrifice in battle. After Shiloh, wrote a captain from Illinois, "all sentimental talk of any easy conquest ceased upon both sides."

While the fighting in the West would hinge on control of the rivers, the key to success belonged to whoever could hold the crucial border states of Kentucky and Missouri. These two were the only slave states beyond the Appalachians that had not declared themselves for one side or the other in the aftermath of the Confederate attack on Fort Sumter. The Eastern holdouts, Maryland and Delaware, were inclined to stay in the United States, and were so close to the centers of Federal power that they were sure to be held in the Union by force if need be. But in Missouri and Kentucky, loyalties were so precariously balanced that the two states could go either way—with momentous results. For one thing, each state had a popula-

Citizen soldiers of the 1st Missouri State Guard wear parade-ground finery in this prewar photograph. When war came, most of these men joined the Confederate army organized by General Sterling Price.

tion of about 1.2 million—larger than that of any Confederate state save Virginia. And if both joined the Confederacy, they would increase its size—and presumably its military manpower—by about 25 per cent.

Of greater importance was the strategic location of the two states. Kentucky dominated the length of the Ohio River and was so situated that if it stayed in the Union the Confederates would almost surely lose neighboring Tennessee. If Kentucky joined the Confederacy, on the other hand, it would imperil the blast furnaces, foundries and rolling mills of Ohio. The Confederate proximity might even threaten the Great Lakes coal and iron-ore traffic, which fed much of Northern industry.

Missouri was, if anything, more crucial than Kentucky. If Missouri "went South," Kentucky would probably follow. A Confederate Missouri would imperil the Union's major routes west—blocking off Kansas and flanking southern Illinois. Most important of all, Missouri dominated the key stretch of the Mississippi, including its vital junction with the Ohio at Cairo on the southernmost tip of Illinois.

In the early months of the War, both the Union and the Confederacy were reluctant to apply pressure on Kentucky for fear of tilting the state into the opposite camp. This was no more than sensible discretion, for self-willed Kentucky was against secession and also against coercing secessionists. In mid-April of 1861, when President Lincoln called for 75,000 volunteers to serve for 90 days, Governor Beriah Magoffin refused to send any Kentucky men to act against the Southern states, and his stand was approved by Unionists and secessionists alike. In the delicately balanced Kentucky legislature, secessionists tried and narrowly failed to call a state convention in which they hoped to sever Kentucky from the Union. Instead, the legislature declared the state's resolve to defend its borders against incursions from either side. That fragile neutrality—"conditional unionism," Lincoln hopefully called it—could not last. But moderates hailed it as at least a temporary defeat for the "destructionists" of both North and South.

In Missouri, the battle between secessionists and Unionists was more bitterly fought from the beginning. The southeastern counties and the extreme northwestern portions of the state, along the Kansas border, were solidly for the South. There guerrilla fighting broke out almost immediately after Lincoln's election in November 1860; plundering bands of "jayhawkers" from the free-soil state of Kansas exchanged raids with slaveholding neighbors across the border, the pro-Southern "border ruffians." All this was merely a continuation of the casual raiding and bloodletting that had made John Brown famous or infamous five years before.

Elsewhere in Missouri, neither Unionists nor secessionists were clearly ahead. In the rich slaveholding counties along the Missouri River, where Southern sentiment was strong, slaveholders were opposed to going to war on the side of the South because they feared that a consequent invasion from the North would destroy the value of slaves as property. Throughout the state, the natural bias of family ties to the South was offset to some degree by the fact that for four decades Missouri had been unusually involved in Federal policy, thanks to its location as the doorway to the great trans-Mississippi West.

And as in Kentucky, Missouri's industry was turned toward the North. Skilled German workers had poured into the state by the tens of thousands. Most of them were liberal-leaning refugees from the 1848 German revolution, which failed to establish constitutional government and a unified national state. Many settled in the thriving river port of St. Louis, which was sometimes referred to as the largest foreign city in the United States. Strongly opposed to slavery, the new workers posed a challenge to the entrenched political leaders, whose sympathies were predominantly with the South.

The Governor of Missouri, Claiborne Fox Jackson, was openly for secession. A noted orator, Jackson made his position clear when Lincoln issued his call for 90-day volunteers. In reply, Jackson unfurled some of his fanciest rhetoric: "Your requisition is illegal, unconstitutional, revolutionary, inhuman, diabolical, and cannot be complied with."

But when it came to actual secession, Jackson found himself frustrated. At a state-wide convention called by the Governor shortly before the outbreak of war, the majority turned out to be Unionist, although cautious enough to vote in favor of neutrality. Jackson dropped the issue and started corresponding with Confederate President Jefferson Davis while awaiting a more favorable turn of events.

Governor Jackson's chief antagonist in the struggle for the minds of Missourians was Frank P. Blair Jr., the 42-year-old Republican Congressman from St. Louis. A volatile, hard-drinking man capable of violent rages, Blair was a member of a famous political family that had helped to found the Republican Party in the decade before the War. His personal ties to Lincoln were reinforced by the fact that his older brother, Montgomery Blair, was serving as

Postmaster General in Lincoln's Cabinet.

Early in the struggle, Blair heard of a secessionist plot to seize the St. Louis Arsenal, a major depot for the Western frontier. The arsenal held 34,000 rifles and muskets, 1,500,000 cartridges, 90,000 pounds of powder and plenty of artillery, and if the secessionists could overpower the handful of troops guarding the arsenal, they could equip an army and control the state.

Making use of his connections in Washington, Blair asked for more troops to guard the arsenal. Soon 80 men arrived from Fort Riley, Kansas, led by Nathaniel Lyon, a wiry little Regular Army captain who had proved to be a skillful, savage Indian fighter and had been promoted for headlong valor in Mexico. Lyon had made himself infamous in the officers' mess at Fort Riley with his tirades against slavery, secessionists and organized religion. An Army doctor once described him as "narrow-minded, mentally unbalanced" and filled with an "anger that was almost insane." The doctor also judged him "honest to the core, truthful and intelligent." Frank Blair, appraising the pugnacious 42-year-old captain, saw in him an ally who was perhaps tough-minded and violent enough to save Missouri for the Union.

To Blair's annoyance, Lyon was not the top-ranking Federal officer in St. Louis. Based in the city was the overall commander in the West, a distinguished old general named William Selby Harney. Blair, convinced that Harney failed to appreciate the secessionist threat, set out to remedy the situation. In late April he prevailed on the War Department to recall General Harney to Washington for consultation, thus leaving Captain Lyon in command of everything in and around St. Louis. Blair even got the War Department to grant Lyon extraordinary powers, permitting him, at his discretion, to enlist up to 10,000 citizens in the Federal service to maintain public order and defend national property.

In fact, a kind of citizens' army known as the Home Guards and numbering more than 7,000 men had already been organized by Frank Blair to offset the secessionist state militia. When Lyon heard at the beginning of May that Governor Jackson had ordered a contingent of 700 state militiamen into spring encampment on the western edge of St. Louis, he summoned the Home Guard into Federal service, deployed several thousand men in the hills around the city and secretly shipped most of the arsenal's con-

Enraged by the shooting of a comrade, Federal troops open fire on pro-Southern rioters at a St. Louis firehouse in mid-June of 1861. The fatal shot that started it all came from the balcony.

tents to a more secure depot in Illinois.

Denying the charge that they were under orders to seize the arsenal, the militiamen insisted they were on a routine training exercise. Lyon had no proof to the contrary, but he was just the man to get it, at whatever cost. Soon after the militiamen arrived, he borrowed a carriage from Frank Blair's mother-in-law, attired himself in a black bombazine dress and sunbonnet, concealed his red beard behind a heavy veil and drove through the "nest of traitors" on a reconnaissance expedition in the guise of a mother visiting her son.

On his return, he reported balefully that he had seen a company street named for Jefferson Davis, Confederate flags flying over some of the tents and militiamen bearing weapons recently plundered from a Federal arsenal in Baton Rouge. That was evidence enough for Blair and Lyon. On May 10, 1861, Lyon surrounded the camp with 3,000 Home Guardsmen and demanded its surrender. The militiamen gave up forthwith.

The episode might have ended there without violence if Lyon had not insisted on making a show to warn the secessionists. Although the militiamen had surrendered peacefully, they refused to swear a loyalty oath, and Lyon decided to march them through the streets to the arsenal as a public humiliation. He formed the Home Guards into two long files, lined up the angry militiamen between them and set off through the streets with drums rolling.

It happened that the Home Guards were almost all German immigrants, known as "die Schwartze Garde" to their friends and as "damned Dutchmen" to their enemies. A crowd hostile to the Germans gathered along the route of march and very soon turned mean. The Home Guards were caught in a barrage of curses and spittle.

Then, at a crowded intersection, stones began to fly. Someone in the crowd emptied a revolver at the soldiers. Several Guardsmen went down, one wounded fatally. The soldiers now lost their heads. Colonel Henry Boernstein, a veteran of the Austrian Army and the editor of a German language newspaper, ordered his men to return the fire. The Guards aimed into the crowd at point-blank range. Scores of people, including women and children, were knocked sprawling.

Matters were now completely out of hand. The mob tore up paving blocks and attacked the soldiers, injuring many. Gunfire on both sides became so heavy that General William Tecumseh Sherman, who happened to be a spectator, recalled running for his life to escape bullets flying from every direction. By the end of the day, 90 civilians in the crowd had been hit and 28 of them were dead or dying. Two of those killed were women and one was a baby in its mother's arms. To avoid inciting the crowd further, Lyon dismissed the Home Guardsmen after they reached the arsenal.

Despite that conciliatory gesture, mobs roamed out of control through the night that followed, and burning buildings lighted the sky. The next day seven more persons were shot to death in clashes with Home Guardsmen who were belatedly sent out to restore order. The deaths in St. Louis—and most especially the poignant image of that baby killed in its mother's arms—destroyed Missouri's hopes of staying neutral.

As the Guardsmen steadily suppressed the rioting, their tough tactics frightened many secessionists, who now fled the city in buggies, on horseback, by train and by the steamboats of the Memphis Packet Company. By the afternoon of May 12, recalled an eyewitness, 3,000 citizens had gone "over the river, down the river, up the river, anywhere to escape the fury of the Dutch." Pro-Confederate resistance in the city had been broken; St. Louis was safe for the Union, and henceforth would serve without incident as headquarters for Federal Army operations in the Western theater.

At midnight, in the state house at Jefferson City, 100-odd miles west of St. Louis, secessionist legislators met in a frenzy. One of them remembered that "many members had belts strapped around their waists and from one to three pistols or bowie knives fastened to them." Expecting Lyon and his men to arrive momentarily, the legislators shouted through a bill giving the government dictatorial powers to raise an army to defend Missouri against attack by United States forces.

As news of the St. Louis "massacre" spread to the western reaches of Missouri, the raids across the Kansas border increased in ferocity, igniting a full-fledged guerrilla war that would rage alongside the regular War for three bloody years. Whole counties on the rural fringes of Missouri would be depopulated by mindless violence.

In the meantime, recruits to the secessionist cause began pouring into Jefferson City. Command of all Missouri troops was given to Brigadier General Sterling "Pap" Price, who was reputed to be the most popular man in the state. A tall, bulky man with a shock of white hair, a loud voice and an easygoing style of leadership, he had been a legislator, governor and U.S. congressman before resigning his Congressional seat in 1844 to form the 2nd Missouri Mounted Volunteers and serve in the Mexican War. His personal popularity was credited with bringing many halfhearted Union men into the Confederate Army.

On June 6, Price and Governor Jackson demanded and received from Lyon—newly appointed a brigadier general—an assurance that they would be "free from molestation" if they wished to travel to St. Louis to meet with Blair and Lyon in a last-minute bid to save the peace. It was a curious, *pro forma* meeting, according to a young Southern journalist named Thomas Snead, who attended as one of the Governor's aides. Neither side seemed to want an accord; in any event, they were much too far apart. Price and Jackson were so openly pro-Southern that their promise not to join the Confederacy in return for formal Federal acceptance of their neutrality looked to the Unionists like a trick. On the other hand, the Governor's party distrusted Blair and Lyon—seeing them as irreconcilably militant and extreme, and intent on forcing down their throats an antislavery, anti-Southern position that violated their sense of loyalty to their state.

Lyon made his position explicit when he rose abruptly after four hours of fruitless discussion. He said: "Rather than concede to the state of Missouri for one single instant the right to dictate to my government in any matter however unimportant"—here he grimly tapped each man on the chest—"I would see you, and you, and you, and you and every man, woman and child in the state dead and buried." Then, adding unnecessarily, "This means war," he walked out, spurs and saber rattling.

Everyone appeared shocked and saddened to see him go. They rose from the table, Snead recalled, and "bade farewell to each

Brigadier General William Harney, the first wartime commander of the U.S. Army in the West, issued the apologetic proclamation at right after 28 pro-Confederate rioters were killed in St. Louis by the Home Guards. Ardent Unionists argued that Harney's efforts to restore peace played into Confederate hands, and they persuaded President Lincoln to replace him.

PROCLAMATION

Military Department of the West,
ST. LOUIS, MAY 12th, 1861.

TO THE PEOPLE
OF THE
STATE OF MISSOURI
AND
CITY OF SAINT LOUIS.

I have just returned to this Post, and have assumed the Military Command of this Department. No one can more deeply regret the deplorable state of things existing here than myself. The past cannot be recalled. I can only deal with the present and the future.

I most anxiously desire to discharge the delicate and onerous duties devolved upon me, so as to preserve the public peace. I shall carefully abstain from the exercise of any unnecessary powers, and from all interference with the proper functions of the public officers of the State and City. I therefore call upon the public authorities and the people to aid me in preserving the public peace.

The Military force stationed in this Department by the Authority of the Government, and now under my command, will only be used in the last resort to preserve the peace. I trust I may be spared the necessity of resorting to martial law, but the public peace MUST BE PRESERVED, and the lives and property of the people protected. Upon a careful review of my instructions, I find I have no authority to change the location of the "Home Guards."

To avoid all cause of irritation and excitement, if called upon to aid the local authorities in preserving the public peace, I shall, in preference, make use of the Regular Army.

I ask the people to pursue their peaceful avocations, and to observe the laws and orders of their local authorities, and to abstain from the excitements of Public Meetings and heated discussions. My appeal, I trust, may not be in vain, and I pledge the Faith of a Soldier to the earnest discharge of my duty.

WILLIAM S. HARNEY.
Brigadier General, U. S. A. Com'g Dept.

other courteously and kindly, and separated—Blair to fight for the Union, we for the land of our birth."

Within four days, Lyon and his Home Guards occupied the Confederate state capital, while General Price, Governor Jackson, assorted legislators and the ragtag makings of an army fled northwest following the course of the Missouri River. On the march, they were joined by 1,500 horse under the command of the dashing border-war cavalry hero Captain Jo Shelby.

By taking Jefferson City, Lyon had not only deprived Jackson's forces of the ma-

chinery of state government but had provided himself with a jumping-off place for the whirlwind campaign he hoped would crush the rebellion before it got organized. He quickly loaded the bulk of his 6,000-man force on river steamers and pushed up the Missouri in hot pursuit of the fleeing Jackson and Price.

Lyon almost cornered the Confederate leaders at Boonville. He landed there in strength and in a sharp skirmish routed the force that had begun to assemble around Price. But the secessionists slipped away to continue their flight.

Outside Boonville, Jackson and Price decided to split up. The plan called for Jackson to fall back toward the southwest, where the Union forces could not pursue by steamboat. Price, accompanied only by his staff and a small escort, would head southwest, too, but at a much faster rate. His mission was to seek reinforcements from General Ben McCulloch, a former Texas Ranger and Mexican War scout who was moving north from Arkansas with a well-trained force of 5,400 men. When Price returned with McCulloch's force, the joint Confederate command would presumably be more than strong enough to turn and fight the pursuing Lyon's 6,000 men.

As war came to Missouri, the overall Federal command in the West passed to a nationally known figure, Major General John Charles Frémont. At the age of 48, Frémont was a volatile, rather romantic man who had made a glamorous reputation for a series of expeditions that mapped the Oregon Trail and the California Trail. In 1856, he had been the first presidential nominee of the Republican Party. He owed his new command partly to

The Missouri Capitol at Jefferson City sits on a bluff above the Missouri River. The legislators meeting here at the start of the War were, for the most part, moderates who hoped to avoid bloodshed through compromise.

the intervention of Frank Blair, whose first choice, Lyon, had been vetoed by Washington because the fierce little general had outraged so many moderate Missourians.

Opposing Frémont as the senior Confederate commander was 55-year-old Major General Leonidas Polk. Trained at West Point—where Jefferson Davis was his friend and classmate—Polk had subsequently taken religious orders in the Episcopal Church and risen to become Bishop of Louisiana. Although Polk was highly regarded by the government in Richmond—President Davis had personally called him back into service—he was thought by some professional military men to be a textbook general who lacked drive and flair.

Frémont and Polk had a good deal in common. Both men were only marginally competent as commanders. Both railed at the shortage of weapons and supplies, complaining that their governments satisfied the needs of the Eastern campaigns first and sent them whatever was left over. The troops they received were—as Frémont griped to the War Department—"entirely unacquainted with the refinements of military exercise." Here, as in the East, the commanders were faced with an enormous training problem. Well-disciplined troops, such as the Federal Home Guard and the Confederate force under Ben McCulloch, were rare exceptions. Until large numbers of the green recruits on both sides could be instructed in the essentials of weaponry and hammered into a semblance of functional regiments and brigades, no large-scale, formal offensive was possible in the West.

In the meantime, the small-scale, irregular war in Missouri picked up momentum as General Lyon's Federals headed south in pursuit of General Price and Governor Jackson. In Lyon's command was a detachment of 1,250 Home Guards led by Colonel Franz Sigel. The colonel was an intense professional soldier who had left his native Germany after fighting with distinction in the failed revolution of 1848. A strict disciplinarian, he had relentlessly drilled the Guardsmen to prepare them for combat. They were thoroughly versed in formation movements, gunnery and small-arms drill.

The Germans had an important role in Lyon's campaign plan. His idea was to detach them from his main force and send them south by rail as part of a 2,500-man expedition to cut off Jackson's retreat toward Arkansas. Reinforced by volunteers who joined him as he marched, Jackson now had about 2,600 infantry, plus the 1,500 cavalry troops brought in by Jo Shelby. If this considerable force could be blocked, Lyon and his main force would have time to come up and attack them from the rear.

The brigade took a train to the rail terminus of Rolla, then marched 125 miles southwest to Springfield. There Sigel left the main body, taking 1,500 of his Germans to reconnoiter as far as the Arkansas line. Returning, he encamped a mile southeast of Carthage on the evening of July 4 and sent his commissary officers into town to arrange for supplies. The officers returned with the exciting news that Governor Jackson was 10 miles to the north and getting ready to move into the town of Carthage.

Sigel knew that he was outnumbered by more than 2 to 1, but he also knew he had no time to send for reinforcements. He gave orders to march against Jackson before dawn.

The two forces met nine miles north of Carthage—at a point where the prairie de-

Let out! General, let out! he's getting close to us.

Oh Govnor Jackson I'm trying all I can to hold in

THE BATTLE OF BOONEVILLE, OR THE GREAT MISSOURI "LYON" HUNT.

A Union cartoon satirizes the rout of Confederate forces at Boonville, Missouri, on June 17, 1861. The two Confederate leaders—Governor Claiborne Jackson, dressed as a woman, and General Sterling Price—flee from a charging lion with the face of Brigadier General Nathaniel Lyon.

scended in a long, gentle slope to a belt of trees skirting Corn Creek and then rose again to a well-rounded ridge. Jackson and his senior officers were confident in their superior numbers and content to wait on the northern ridge while the Germans descended the opposite slope and crossed through the trees.

As the Germans emerged from the woods, they deployed in column of companies to forestall any flanking movement by cavalry—a precision maneuver that the raw Confederates watched with admiration. At 700 yards, Sigel's artillery opened fire, and the Confederate artillery replied.

After an hour of ineffectual artillery dueling, the Federal infantry surged forward

in line of battle behind such accurate rifle fire that the center of the Confederate line showed signs of buckling. But then Confederate cavalrymen swept away to the south and disappeared into the woods at the rear. The cavalry made no attempt to attack the well-defended Federal right or left flanks, but Sigel became worried that he might be cut off from his lumbering wagon train. He ordered a retreat under fire. His men carried out that famously difficult maneuver with brilliance, moving their cannon back one by one in a sort of leapfrog movement to provide covering fire for the infantry.

It was an inconclusive little battle with not many casualties—the Federals lost 13 killed and the Confederates 10. But it served as a temporary check to the fleeing Confederates, and it raised Lyon's hopes that he would eventually be able to catch and destroy them. In addition, it was richly instructive to the local Confederate commanders, who saw for the first time the importance of formal training. When news of the battle and the Germans' maneuvers reached Price, he realized that the need for seasoned troops to support Jackson was even more urgent than he had thought. He hastened on south toward his rendezvous with McCulloch.

Price's command grew as he went. From Missouri's farms, forests and villages, recruits by the hundreds came swarming to join Pap's crusade. He would take only those who brought their own horses. The rest he told to wait for Governor Jackson, who would be passing with his infantry columns in a few days' time.

Price's efforts to train and outfit his growing force seemed doomed to fail. The farm boys and backwoodsmen who streamed into his command as he moved south were irregular and ill equipped in every way. The weapons they carried ranged from shotguns and squirrel rifles to ancient flintlock fowling pieces. None of them had uniforms or tents or supplies. They made their own ammunition, using lead from southern Missouri mines and molds fashioned from green hardwood. "My first cartridge resembled a turnip," recalled a recruit—but soon, he added, his unit's homemade ammunition looked almost professional. One-inch slugs cut from iron rods or old chains furnished the artillery with canister, and smooth stones took the place of solid shot. However, the troops had no waterproof cartridge boxes, and since water would ruin their paper cartridges,

they were unable to march in rainy weather.

This motley force slowly rambled southward, bivouacking in the open, living off the land and foraging the horses on prairie grass. By the time Price got to southwestern Missouri, he had 1,200 men; his command increased to 7,000 men on July 7, when he met and took over Jackson's infantrymen. Nearly a third of the men were without weapons; they were told to arm themselves in battle by the gruesome but practical procedure of following on the heels of their armed comrades and seizing weapons from the hands of the dead and dying.

On the 29th of July, 23 days after the Carthage battle and about 40 miles to the southeast, Price linked up with the little army of Ben McCulloch. Price was disgusted to find that the Texan was a vain, flamboyant man who wore a velvet suit with flowing swallowtails. McCulloch in turn deprecated Price as "nothing but an old militia general" and cast grave doubts on the fighting ability of Price's "half-starved infantry" and "huckleberry cavalry." But now at last, with a joint command of 14,000 men, including some last-minute reinforcements, the Confederate leaders had strength to attack Lyon.

In fact, Lyon was in poor and worsening shape. His effective force was rapidly dwindling to less than 6,000 as the enlistment period of 90-day volunteers came to an end and many returned home. And while pursuing Price, Lyon had seriously overextended himself. He had moved a full 120 miles beyond the railroad at Rolla, his only dependable source of supply, and was camped near the town of Springfield, Missouri, roughly 50 miles north of the Price-McCulloch rendezvous.

Price wanted to attack Lyon immediately,

The 12th Wisconsin Volunteer Infantry stands in line beyond its regimental band (*center*) as the 16th Wisconsin (*right*) marches up in column on the parade ground at Camp Randall in Madison, Wisconsin.

Marching two abreast, the nearly 1,000 men of the 12th Wisconsin Volunteers wind their way past a wood between Quincy, Illinois, and Hannibal, Missouri.

The Marchingest Outfit in the U.S. Army

When the recruits of the 12th Wisconsin Volunteer Infantry were sent to Missouri in January 1862, they fully expected to see plenty of action in the strife-torn state. Instead, as shown in these watercolors by a corporal named John Gaddis, they billeted in the town of Weston in northwestern Missouri and found to their disappointment that the area was utterly peaceful. And so for a month, before moving on, they drilled and stood guard and marched about, looking in vain for a wholesome fight.

Their marching turned out to be an omen of sorts. Though the outfit later got into interesting campaigns, the men spent most of their time marching from post to post. In three years, they hiked an estimated 3,380 miles, making them the marchingest regiment in the Federal Army.

Encamped at Weston, Missouri, a soldier stops to greet Company E's mascot—a young bear. The bear marched alongside the men and lived in a box with a hole sawed out for a door.

On a frigid January night, men of the 12th Wisconsin huddle about huge bonfires on the banks of the Mississippi opposite Hannibal, Missouri. They had just completed a 22-mile march in six hours.

but McCulloch flatly refused to put his troops under Price's command. Price, desperate to destroy Lyon's army and swing Missouri to the Confederacy, confronted McCulloch in a stormy session and offered to give him the command if he would agree to attack. On that understanding, the merged forces moved north. They went into camp at Wilson's Creek, about 10 miles from Springfield; McCulloch picked the spot because nearby fields of ripening corn could feed his ragged army.

Lyon realized he was in a difficult spot. He knew that the Confederates were preparing to attack him, and that they outnumbered him by more than 2 to 1. On the other hand, he could scarcely retreat, for he had virtually no cavalry to protect his straggling column from the blows of the Confederate mounted troops.

Lyon decided to make an overnight march to Wilson's Creek and hit the enemy at dawn, relying on surprise to offset the Confederate advantage in numbers. Just before dark on August 9, he was visited in his tent by Colonel Sigel. The colonel wanted to take a column on a wide sweep to the south and come in on the Confederate right flank and rear while Lyon with the main force was striking from the north against the Confederate left. Lyon agreed and gave Sigel 1,200 men and a battery of artillery.

Making a tour of his encampment, Lyon briefly addressed his troops. He told them to hold their fire until the enemy got close and to aim low to counter the recoil of their muskets. Above all, they were not to be frightened: "It is no part of a soldier's duty to get scared." Shortly after dark, Sigel marched out at the head of his column. Lyon swung into the saddle of his gray stallion and

Home Guards led by Colonel Franz Sigel intercept Governor Jackson's Confederate troops retreating south from Boonville at a stream near Carthage on July 5, 1861. After a lively artillery duel, the aggressive but outnumbered Federals were pushed aside and the Confederates completed their retreat into southwestern Missouri.

followed with the bulk of the army. In theory, he should have had more than 4,000 men left after Sigel's departure; in fact, sickness and the necessity of posting a guard detachment in Springfield left Lyon with a main force of only about 3,600 men. The night was humid and oppressive, and about midnight it began to rain.

Wilson's Creek was an abysmal place to fight a battle. The creek, curving west and south toward the James River, passed between steeply rising bluffs and tall hills cut by ravines. The Confederate encampments were strung out for approximately two miles on either side of the point where Wilson's Creek was intersected by the main road from Springfield. On the west side of the creek, from which Lyon's forces were approaching, there arose a 150-foot spur of land that would soon become known as Bloody Hill. The hill overlooked a wilderness of rambling streams, rocky outcroppings and heavy growths of brush and scrub oak. The area in which the two armies would clash was cramped—barely 520 yards long by 175 yards wide.

Approaching this terrain, Lyon was favored by a stroke of luck. It was raining hard, and the Confederate commanders had placed their pickets and foragers under shelter at midnight so they could keep their ammunition dry. As a result, the Confederates failed to detect Sigel's stealthy flanking movement, and they did not discover Lyon's columns until shortly after dawn.

As soon as Lyon saw that he was detected, he deployed his troops, threw out skirmishers and advanced at the double up the northern slope of Bloody Hill, toward a plateau where a 600-man Confederate detachment waited. The Confederates, who were armed with shotguns, could not stand up to the rifled muskets of Lyon's troops. They fell back first to the crest of the hill and then to its southern slope.

To the south, Sigel's men waited behind a screen of dense woods, their guns trained on the encampment of a Confederate regiment from Arkansas that lay only 500 yards away. At the boom of guns to the north, Sigel's artillery opened up. The surprised Arkansas troops found shells bursting among their cook fires and "literally ran out from under" the barrage, as one of them put it.

Price was sharing a breakfast of soggy corn bread and tough beef with Thomas Snead, who had left the Governor's staff and was now a colonel serving as Price's adjutant. McCulloch and another officer joined them. They had all started eating when a Missourian galloped up, shouting that Lyon was within a mile of the camp. McCulloch, still convinced the Missourians were panicky amateurs, snapped, "That's not true!" Then a shell came screaming into the camp from the north, and in a minute they heard Sigel's fire to the south. Price ran to his horse to meet Lyon's attack, while McCulloch took charge of the threat to the south.

The battle thus joined was a nightmare of blundering maneuver. On the southern slope of Bloody Hill, the two armies struggled clumsily and savagely to gain control of the summit. The opposing lines were less than 300 yards apart, but the scrub concealed them from each other. For hours on end, Thomas Snead wrote, "the lines would approach again and again within less than fifty yards of each other and then, after delivering a deadly fire, each would fall back a few paces to reform and reload, only to advance again, and again re-

Unfriendly allies, General Sterling Price (*left*) and Brigadier General Ben McCulloch cooperated unwillingly in the struggle for Missouri. Price would have preferred to make do without McCulloch's help, and McCulloch, ordered to defend Arkansas and the Indian Territory, grudgingly went to aid Price at Jefferson Davis' request.

new this strange battle in the woods." What haunted him most was "the deep silence which now and then fell upon the smoking field" while "the two armies, unseen of each other, lay but a few yards apart, gathering strength to grapple again in the death struggle for Missouri."

Lyon's men, hearing the firing to the south die away, waited with increasing anxiety for Sigel's men to sweep up the south slope of Bloody Hill and take the Confederates from the rear. But Sigel was in trouble. After his original surprise attack had overwhelmed the Confederate encampments in front of him, he had continued circling to his right, across an open meadow, until he had moved nearly three quarters of the way around the Confederate army. At this point, he was intercepted by McCulloch, who had hurriedly formed a force from elements of the 1st Arkansas Mounted Riflemen and the

This crude map of the Battle of Wilson's Creek, torn from the sketch pad of a magazine artist with General Lyon's army, shows the Federal forces, represented by white bars, attacking the Confederates, shown as dark bars, above the point where the Fayetteville-Springfield road crosses the creek, which is indicated by a wavy line. The X below Totten's battery, at upper left, marks the spot where Lyon was killed.

3rd Louisiana Infantry, including the well-known Pelican Rifles.

Sigel then learned at great cost that neither side had standard uniform colors this early in the War. He saw a mass of gray-clad men approaching and mistook them for the men of the 1st Iowa Infantry, who wore gray. He passed the word along his line not to fire and sent out a corporal to verify the identity of the approaching troops.

Seeing this man come near, McCulloch asked him which outfit he was with. "Sigel's regiment," replied the corporal—and then, as if realizing the situation, raised his rifle to fire at McCulloch. Before he could pull the trigger, Corporal Henry Gentles of the Pelican Rifles shot him dead. McCulloch swiveled in his saddle and shouted to the Pelicans' commanding officer, "Captain, take your company up and give them hell!"

As the Confederates charged in a howling frontal attack, Arkansas and Missouri batteries on the hills to the east and west opened fire, enfilading Sigel's lines and spreading what he described as "confusion and frightful consternation." The Federal soldiers broke and ran, leaving behind five cannon. Sigel managed to get back to Springfield with a small escort.

Now the whole Confederate army turned on Lyon's depleted force. "The engagement at once became general and almost inconceivably fierce along the entire line," recalled Major J. M. Schofield, Lyon's chief of staff. Men fought blindly, scarcely knowing what they were doing. Major Schofield came across one soldier loading and reloading as if in a trance and firing straight up into the air. Noticing something familiar about the screech of incoming shells, Lyon's troops realized that the Confederates had turned Si-

Toppling from his horse, General Lyon falls mortally wounded at Wilson's Creek, Missouri, on August 10, 1861, in a sketch *(left)* by newspaper artist Henri Lovie. In the published engraving *(below)*, Lyon is restored to his horse and leads the 1st Iowa Regiment into the battle. The reason for the change: The newspaper had already published a rendering of Lyon's death and the editor decided against duplication.

gel's guns on them—and that the flanking attack had failed. Over the din of battle, a Confederate commander shouted to his troops to aim for the belly; a man died slowly from such a wound, giving him time to meet his maker. Troops on both sides fell in such numbers that the Federal artillery commanders had to clear a path through the dead and wounded when they wanted to move their guns.

The fight on Bloody Hill raged for five hours. At the end of that time, the sheer weight of Confederate numbers began to tell, and the Union line seemed about to buckle. Yet the regular Federal batteries still dominated the field, breaking up every Confederate attack. While trying to rally his faltering forces, Lyon was wounded in the head and the leg by fragments from a bursting shell. He "walked on," said a Federal officer who was near him, "waving his sword and hallooing." But the general looked white and shaky, and the officer noticed that "suddenly blood appeared on the side of his head." Dazed, Lyon walked a few yards toward the rear and muttered to his adjutant that he feared "the day is lost."

Yet he roused himself again, mounted a horse and led one more charge at the head of a Kansas unit. As Lyon galloped over the crest of Bloody Hill, a bullet took him full in the chest and knocked him off his horse. His orderly, a 1st Cavalry regular named Albert Lehman, held him in his arms. "Lehman," said the general, "I am killed."

With Lyon's death, the battle dwindled; both sides had fought to exhaustion. The Federals discovered that they had no officer left above the rank of major to take over the command. Slowly, the two armies disengaged; the Federals fell back toward

Springfield, and the Confederates were too spent to follow. "We watched the retreating enemy through our field glasses," recalled a Confederate general, "and were glad to see him go."

Casualties were awesome: 1,317 for the Federal troops, of whom 258 were killed outright, and 1,336 on the Confederate side, with 281 killed. The casualty rate for the Federals was an appallingly high 27 per cent—three times that of the Confederates—but even that figure scarcely suggested the devastation of rifle fire and cannon fire delivered at point-blank range. Several infantry regiments on both sides had casualty rates as high as 33 per cent.

The battle was counted a victory for the Confederates, for they remained in possession of the field. But in time it became obvious that even if Lyon had lost a battle he had accomplished much of what he set out to do. His aggressive pursuit of Price had driven the Missouri Confederates into the hinterlands, kept them off-balance and left Unionists free to consolidate their position. In the wake of Lyon's seizure of Jefferson City, a Unionist convention had met to declare state offices vacant and to appoint a loyal governor and other state officials. That put the machinery of government back in Union hands, and the centers of population and industry remained under Federal control.

For all that, the loss of Lyon left a serious gap in Federal leadership and intensified Washington's growing dissatisfaction with the command situation in the West. General Frémont had started well, announcing an ambitious plan for raising a huge army and moving it down the Mississippi, escorted by a fleet of gunboats. Whoever held the Missis-

Smoke rings the Federal fort at Lexington, Missouri, as one wave of attackers *(right)* is repulsed and another forms *(foreground)*. The Federal troops, shielded by massive earthen ramparts, withstood such assaults for eight days before surrendering on September 20, 1861.

sippi, he had proclaimed, "would hold the country by the heart." As a preliminary step, he had ordered 38 armored mortar boats to supplement the fleet of gunboats that the Navy had already contracted for.

But Frémont was better at making grandiose plans than he was at executing them. He also had a weakness for pomp and turned his headquarters in St. Louis into a place that gave bewildered visitors the impression they had wandered into a European court. To guard his privacy, he formed an elite force of 300 Kentuckians averaging 5 feet 11½ inches in height and 40½ inches around the chest. He had an affinity for foreign adventurers and filled his personal staff with illegally commissioned Hungarians and Italians decked out in feathers and gold loops of the kind Missourians called "chicken guts."

Frémont also surrounded himself with old cronies so notably venal that the head of a Congressional investigating committee called them "a gang of California robbers and scoundrels." Military men who urgently needed to see him found it "more trouble," as one colonel put it, "than it would be to get an audience with the Czar of Russia." The colonel was kept waiting six hours. Then, before being admitted to Frémont's presence, he was sent back to his quarters to change to dress uniform.

Shortly after the Federals were checked at Wilson's Creek, Frémont made a major political blunder. In an effort to control the guerrilla warfare raging in southern Missouri, he placed the state under martial law. His proclamation ordered the summary execution of men caught in arms against the Union, and the immediate freeing of slaves.

The edict was a double error. The threat of execution invited retaliation—as one of the

state's most daring guerrilla leaders quickly made clear. This was Jeff Thompson, a transplanted Virginian who had recruited and trained his irregulars in the swampy wilderness around the southeastern Missouri river town of New Madrid. He styled himself the "Missouri Swamp Fox" and affectionately called his barefoot recruits the "swamp rats." If Frémont carried out his threat, said Thompson in his own proclamation, he would "hang, draw and quarter a minion of said Abraham Lincoln" for every secessionist executed.

Frémont's order freeing the slaves threatened to cause even more mischief. Lincoln had a political purpose to serve in his insistence that this was a war to preserve the Union rather than one to extinguish slavery: He wished to quiet the fears and retain the loyalty of slaveowners in the vital border states. With all that thrown into jeopardy by

Frémont's emancipation proclamation, he quickly wrote to the general "in a spirit of caution, and not of censure" and expressed concern over the likely alienation of powerful elements in the border regions. He asked Frémont voluntarily to withdraw the proclamation. Stubbornly Frémont refused to "change or shade it." Lincoln then ordered it withdrawn. Frémont's days in the Western command were numbered.

Meanwhile Frémont had to contend with another campaign by General Price, who struck north again just a month after Wilson's Creek. This time Price attacked without Ben McCulloch, who had taken his tough little army back to Arkansas. The new offensive started in Springfield, which Price had occupied after Lyon's shattered force withdrew, and his objective was the town of Lexington, located on the Missouri River about 125 miles northwest of Springfield.

Driven from their farms in southern Missouri by Confederate troops, pro-Union homesteaders encamp near Rolla in the winter of 1861. Many of the refugees headed for St. Louis, where Federal authorities forced Southern sympathizers to underwrite the cost of caring for them.

Because Lexington was an overland freight depot and the most important center of population between St. Louis and Kansas City, Price regarded it as an important first step in repossessing Missouri.

Even without McCulloch, Price's command had now increased to approximately 10,000 men—far more than Frémont felt able to spare for the defense of western Missouri. Defending Lexington was a force of about 3,000 men bivouacked inside earthworks surrounding the campus of white-pillared Masonic College. The battle for the town raged around the fortifications for almost nine broiling-hot days as Price surrounded the Union troops and gradually drew his lines tighter and tighter. At one point the Confederates cleverly advanced behind a moving breastwork of wet hemp bales that protected them even from artillery fire.

The Federal men kept up the fight, but with dwindling enthusiasm and increasing thirst. Cut off from the river and other water sources, convinced that Frémont was not coming to their aid, they finally surrendered on September 20. Price's army captured a commissary full of desperately needed supplies, together with 215 horses, 100 wagons, five pieces of artillery and 3,000 muskets.

The news of the Federal defeat, coming so soon after Wilson's Creek, shocked the North and further weakened the precarious position of Frémont, who was blamed for not having relieved the Lexington garrison. Although Frémont defended himself vigorously—he even shut down the St. Louis *Evening News* for criticizing him—he realized full well that only a military victory could save him. He wrote General Winfield Scott that he was "taking the field myself and hope to destroy the enemy." Scott replied tersely that the President "expects you to repair the disaster at Lexington without loss of time."

Frémont marched southwest with a new army of 50,000 men. By the end of October he was just 60 miles north of Springfield, which was defended by only a token force of Confederates. Frémont's Kentucky bodyguard led the cavalry and took the town in a headlong charge that carried them through the outlying picket lines and into the courthouse square almost before the Confederates realized they were under attack.

Here Frémont's offensive stalled. His reconnaissance was so poor that he believed the bulk of Price's force was only nine miles away, near Wilson's Creek again. In fact, Price was easily 50 miles away, near the town of Neosho, to which he had retreated from Lexington on learning that Frémont was on the march.

While Frémont was preparing to assault an army far beyond his reach, Lincoln concluded that the general was "the prey of wicked and designing men" and that he had "absolutely no military capacity." Winfield Scott relieved Frémont of his command.

Just before Frémont disappeared from the scene, he performed an important service for the Federal army in the West. He needed a man to command the troops assembling at Cairo, Illinois, for future offensives to the south. The last officer he interviewed was a scruffy little brigadier general who had left the Regular Army seven years earlier under a cloud and had spent months trying to find his way into the War. Frémont was impressed by the brigadier's "dogged persistence" and "iron will." So he gave the Cairo command to Ulysses S. Grant.

General Grant's Strategic Mudhole

Cairo, Illinois, the headquarters and staging area of a new Federal army, had the raw look and racy atmosphere of a frontier boom town when General Ulysses S. Grant took command in September of 1861.

The small civilian population—2,200 in 1860—had already been inundated with 8,000 soldiers, and more troops kept arriving by riverboat and railroad to drill at Fort Defiance and Camp Smith. The town's tenderloin, which had for decades catered to rivermen pausing here at the strategic confluence of the Mississippi and Ohio Rivers, expanded apace of the military influx. Captain J. S. Hacker called the wartime town "hell-roaring Cairo" and noted that "the many places of amusement, gambling and worse kept the Provost Marshall busy and the Guard House full."

With few recorded exceptions, the incoming troops took an immediate dislike to Cairo that soon ripened into revulsion. The climate was humid; rats and mosquitoes spread diseases; and the tenderloin operators cheated and even robbed many soldiers. Worst of all, periodic flooding turned the town's unpaved streets and the troops' bivouacs into seas of mud. Wrote a young volunteer from Wisconsin: "I have witnessed hogpens that are palaces compared with our situation here."

These abominable conditions did have one beneficial effect; they encouraged soldiers to train hard for an invasion of the South. Indeed, a private reported, "Nothing would suit them better."

Docking at Cairo, the steamboat *Aleck Scott* delivers hundreds of Federal soldiers to local camps for training. Most of the regiments that were stationed at Cairo came from other parts of Illinois, and a few were from the neighboring states of Wisconsin, Indiana and Ohio.

The Illinois Central Railroad runs parallel to Cairo's main street (left) and the Ohio River, where floating warehouses lie moored to the levee. The railroad collected troops and supplies en route south from its point of origin in Chicago.

On Cairo's Commercial Avenue (*right*), Koehler's gunshop, Dinkel's saloon, Schenk's drugstore and other crude frame buildings line a boardwalk along the muddy thoroughfare. During the spring flood in 1862 (*above*), the streets lay submerged, and steam pumps were set up on the levee to carry the floodwaters back to the Ohio River.

CITY GUN SHOP

Fort Defiance, hurriedly built at Cairo in 1861, guards the strategic point of land where the Ohio River empties into the Mississippi. Inside the fort (*inset*), Federal

gunners drill with their 32-pounder cannon and stand watch against a Confederate attack that would never come.

The Go-ahead General

"General Grant is decidedly unmartial in appearance. But it is possible he may figure prominently in action before many weeks."

THOMAS W. KNOX, *NEW YORK HERALD*

2

Ulysses S. Grant began the War as a failure, burdened with the reputation of a drunkard who had resigned from the Army under pressure seven years before. Afterward, when he was famous, his neighbors in Galena, Illinois, spoke of the blankness they had seen in his eyes as he trudged off each morning to clerk in a family leather-goods store and trudged home again at night. He had none of the entrepreneurial sense that might have made him a success in business, but he did have—as he may not himself have recognized until he got an opportunity to use it—high intelligence, a great capacity for military organization and administration, and a taste for fighting. He was, in short, a natural general.

In an age of fiery, flamboyant commanders, Grant was calm, restrained, almost self-effacing. "He was plain, very plain," the Governor of Illinois remembered later, and his soldiers called him "the quiet man." They liked him because he cared about them, he understood the worth of the volunteer soldier, he got things done and he was always ready to fight, which was, after all, the point of the whole thing. He was direct and aggressive, he gave clear commands for which he was willing to take responsibility, and he believed in the attack. He did not like waiting. Every extra day of preparation that he gave his own men, he gave the enemy, too. His principles of war were simple, and he expressed them simply: "Find out where your enemy is, get at him as soon as you can and strike him as hard as you can, and keep moving on."

His real name was Hiram Ulysses Grant, but when he arrived at West Point in 1839 as an undersized 17-year-old, a confusion of records caused him to be listed as Ulysses S. and he left the name so. "I did not take hold of my studies with avidity," Grant wrote. He finished his schooling at the Military Academy near the middle of his class. But he came to know, and to estimate shrewdly, many men who would be his fellow officers and his enemies.

The Mexican War had a profound effect on Grant. When he first heard the sound of guns rumbling in the distance, he wished that he had not joined the Army. But he soon found war wildly stimulating. He was then a regimental quartermaster, whose duties normally kept him behind the lines, but again and again he managed to find his way into combat. Once, poking about the front, he heard the order for a charge and, "lacking the moral courage to return to the camp, charged with the regiment." As American troops started the final assault on Mexico City, Grant once again escaped his quartermaster duties. Moving forward under heavy fire, he and a handful of men saw a church belfry near enemy lines, hoisted a howitzer into it and cleared the way for the advance. That feat earned him promotion to brevet (acting) captain.

After the Mexican War Grant married Julia Dent, sister of a West Point roommate,

Brigadier General Ulysses S. Grant wears his new dress uniform and a recently cultivated square-cut beard in this photograph taken in October 1861.

and soon they had children. But orders took him to California, where his salary could not possibly support his beloved wife and family, and he had to leave them behind. Hoping to make extra money, he engaged in one business venture after another on the West Coast, but all of them failed. Lonely, serving on a remote post under a martinet, feeling a failure, he was overtaken by despair and began to drink. Whether drink impaired his military efficiency remained unproved. But a rumor swept through the small and gossipy peacetime Army: Grant was a drunk. In 1854—to escape a court-martial, some said —he resigned from the Army.

Fifteen years in the Army thus went for nothing, and Grant's next seven were so devastating as to make his Army career bright by comparison. He tried farming and failed. He cut wood to sell on the streets of St. Louis and made an average income of only $48 a month for one year. At Christmas, 1857, he pawned his gold watch for $22. A relative gave him a job in St. Louis as a bill collector, a rough role for which he was hopelessly unsuited. At last, desperate, he appealed to his father, a comfortable tanner, who sent him to Galena to work as a clerk in a leather store operated by Grant's brother. Grant was there, blank-eyed and nearly 39, when the Civil War began.

Galena organized a company of soldiers. The men asked Grant for advice, and as he put it, "I never went into our leather store after that meeting, to put up a package or do other business." He refused command of the company—with a great army abuilding, surely he was to be more than a company commander. But he traveled with the Galena men to the encampment at Springfield, Illinois, where troops poured in to be formed into regiments. Confusion was fearsome and

A fabled horseman, Captain Ulysses S. Grant braves enemy fire in a race to fetch ammunition during the Mexican War. He recalled in his memoirs: "I adjusted myself on the side of my horse furthest from the enemy and with only one foot holding to the cantle of the saddle, and an arm over the neck of the horse exposed, I started at a full run."

Governor Richard Yates pressed Grant into service as a mustering officer. Immediately, the Governor noted, the situation began to smooth out.

Grant was determined to settle for no less than a colonelcy, but he wanted an appointment. As an old regular, he could not bear the idea of standing for election to the command of a volunteer regiment. No appointment was forthcoming, however. He went to St. Louis and renewed his acquaintance with Captain Nathaniel Lyon and met Frank Blair, yet nothing came of his visit. He swallowed his pride and went to Major General George B. McClellan, a junior classmate at West Point who now commanded the Department of the Ohio; he waited two days, but McClellan did not see him. Despairing again, Grant went back to Springfield. The bottle tempted him; as a friend put it, "whenever he was idle and depressed, this appetite came upon him." Then Governor Yates offered rescue: Would Grant accept appointment to the command of the 21st Illinois, then in a state of riotous mutiny against its incompetent elected colonel?

From this dubious start, Grant began a steady climb. He was in his element, he seemed to know just what to do, and he did it with an easy authority that could not be overlooked. First, the regiment. He took over quietly, but "in a very few days," one of his soldiers wrote, "he reduced matters in camp to perfect order." Grant said later that it was "hard work for a few days," but he knew that men want discipline, and he gave it to them with a combination of stern authority and leavening common sense. When the 21st was ordered to northern Missouri to deal with secessionist guerrillas, it marched the 100 miles to the Mississippi instead of going by

rail, and that sort of testing march had a marvelous way of turning men into soldiers.

In Missouri, Grant immediately received an important lesson in command. He led his regiment against a guerrilla force headed by Colonel Thomas Harris of the Missouri Confederates. After a march of 25 miles, Grant started up a hill, beyond which he expected to find Harris and his men drawn up to fight. "My heart kept getting higher and higher," he wrote, "until it felt to me as though it was in my throat. I would have given anything then to have been back in Illinois." Grant had proved his personal courage in Mexico, but this was different: This was command courage. He lacked, or so he said, "the moral courage to halt and consider what to do; I kept right on." The regiment came over the hill to an anticlimax—Harris had fled the spot. "My heart resumed its place," Grant wrote. "It occurred to me at once that Harris had been as much afraid of me as I had been of him. This was a view of the question I had never taken before; but it was one that I never forgot afterwards."

Grant's move on Harris also reflected what would become his dominant trait as a general. "One of my superstitions," he wrote of his boyhood, "had always been when I started to go anywhere or to do anything, not to turn back or to stop until the thing was accomplished." The go-ahead boy was maturing into the go-ahead general.

Grant's handling of the 21st Illinois impressed both Governor Yates and a powerful Illinois Congressman, Elihu Washburne, who also happened to be from Galena, and when the state was allowed to name four brigadiers to the new volunteer army, Grant was among them. He moved up to brigade command with the same easy authority;

General John Frémont gave him a military district embracing the southern tip of Illinois and southeastern Missouri.

From his headquarters at Cairo, at the critical confluence of the Mississippi and Ohio Rivers, Grant showed his propensity for action. Quickly he occupied Paducah, Kentucky, at the mouth of the Tennessee River invasion route, to counter the movement of General Leonidas Polk's Confederate troops into Columbus, Kentucky, 40 miles away. Grant saw the value of Columbus, where guns mounted on the bluff could block the river, and he asked General Frémont for authority to attack immediately. But no orders

came. Columbus was vulnerable then; by November the Confederates had fortified it heavily and it would be harder to take.

Grant's readiness to attack Paducah had made him popular with his men, and they were eager to follow him into battle. Their eagerness persisted in spite of the discouraging kind of operation he now mounted time and again. These were demonstrations—feints designed to keep the enemy guessing—and they meant marching about in the mud for days with no action and seemingly nothing accomplished.

On the 1st of November, Grant received orders for yet another demonstration. General Frémont, in the final stages of his ill-

The musicians of the 21st Illinois Volunteers, Ulysses S. Grant's first Civil War command, put up a bold front of brass and drums. But Grant disliked music intensely and, it was said, would go a mile out of his way to avoid listening to a band.

In this photograph of the Cairo, Illinois, post office, two of the bystanders are thought to be Generals Grant (hands in pockets) and John McClernand (at his left). The picture was taken in September 1861, soon after both men arrived in the vital Ohio River port. They were still in mufti, while waiting for their new brigadier general's uniforms to be sent from New York.

fated campaign against Missouri General Sterling Price, had wanted a show that would hold the Confederates at Columbus in place.

Grant elected to demonstrate against Belmont, a three-shack hamlet across the Mississippi River from Columbus. On November 6, he embarked with 3,114 men on transports, escorted by two wooden gunboats of the Federal river navy. On the evening of November 6, the boats tied up about six miles north of Belmont.

When Polk learned of the Federal approach, he thought it was a feint to disguise an attack on Columbus itself, which was the obvious prize. He sent Brigadier General Gideon Pillow with about 2,700 men to Belmont to meet the feint and held his main force ready to defend his Columbus fortress.

Grant, meanwhile, made an aggressive decision: He would attack Belmont at dawn. By 8:30 a.m. on November 7 his men were ashore three miles above Belmont—and Pillow had completed his crossing and was leading his men to meet the Federals. Grant posted a regiment to guard his transports and ordered the rest of his force forward.

In the lead was a company of the 22nd Illinois under Captain John Seaton, who specialized in skirmish-line tactics. Seaton took his duties very seriously, and about 1,000 feet into the woods, he halted his men and made a speech. A battle loomed, he said. "Many of us have seen the sun rise for the last time. I do not know what the crucial test may cause, but—if I should show the white feather, shoot me dead in my tracks and my family will feel that I died for my country."

In the woods ahead, Confederate muskets rattled and three of Seaton's men went down. "I never thought of running," Captain John Rawlins, Grant's adjutant, wrote

his mother of this, his initiation to combat. But "any man with half a soul must be somewhat brave on the battlefield." The desire to win was stronger than fear for oneself.

As the battle turned this way and that, Seaton found himself behind the 7th Iowa, which, taking a Confederate charge, broke backward "like the opening of a double gate." The Confederates crashed through the opening and Seaton threw his men at them headlong and drove them back.

"They opposed us step by step," Seaton wrote, but his men forced back the enemy "from tree to tree." Grant was at the front, rallying his troops. His mount was shot. He took an aide's horse and galloped forward.

Now the Federals were advancing steadily. After about four hours of battle, the Union troops drove the Confederates back into their camp. There resistance broke. The Confederates scattered and ran for the shelter of the high riverbanks.

Grant's men concluded that they had won and erupted in an unruly celebration. Officers galloped about making victory speeches while soldiers looted Confederate supplies. Bandsmen who had managed to bring their instruments through the fire struck up patriotic airs. "I, myself," said Seaton, "mounted a captured gun, and had the boys join with song in the performance of the band."

Across the river in Columbus, General Polk was surprised to find no attack developing on his main position, so he laid heavy cannon fire on the Federals in Belmont and sent several regiments to land between them and their boats. The Federals' celebration turned suddenly to panic. Some of the officers thought surrender was the only answer. "Well," Grant said calmly, "we must cut our way out as we cut our way in."

A painting of Leonidas Polk stresses his double role as Bishop of Louisiana and general in the Confederate Army. He wears his priestly robes, holds his sword and stands beside a chair draped with his uniform tunic.

The Federals fought their way back to the river and scrambled down the steep bluff in the face of brisk Confederate fire from a wood overlooking the anchorage. Federal details carried wounded men from the battlefield onto the waiting riverboats, and the captains ordered the mooring lines cast off.

Grant was nearly left behind. He wrote: "The captain of a boat that had just pushed out recognized me and ordered the engineer not to start the engine; he then had a plank run out for me. My horse seemed to take in the situation. He put his fore feet over the bank without hesitation or urging, and, with his hind feet well under him, slid down the bank and trotted on board."

The Federals had been driven away, and the Confederates counted Belmont their victory. In fact, neither side had won or lost. It was a pointless battle fought for worthless ground at the cost of some 600 casualties on each side. But it did buck up Federal morale and mark an important distinction about Grant. In a period when generals on both sides felt unready to meet the enemy and Lincoln was growing desperate for action, Grant showed himself willing to fight. The point would not be lost on the President.

At the dining table the night after the battle, Grant hardly spoke. Seaton, who was eating four places from him, wrote later, "We thought he was hard-hearted, cold and indifferent, but it was only the difference between a *real* soldier and amateur soldiers."

On the Confederate side, the situation in the West was growing critical by early autumn of 1861. Nearly everything—arms, men, matériel—was in short supply. An aide later summed up the predicament that faced the man who now became the supreme Confed-

The West's Makeshift Weapons

In the early months of the War, the armies that mustered in the Western theater had to make do with a miscellany of old firearms left over after Washington and Richmond had satisfied the needs of forces closer to home. Most of the soldiers in both armies received muskets that had been manufactured as flintlocks in the 1820s and later converted to percussion. The modification was made by cutting away part of the lock mechanism—the pan that held the priming powder and the flint striker, or frizzen—and by welding a percussion nipple and bolster over the vent. The cock, designed to hold a piece of flint, was replaced by a simple hammer.

Other volunteers were issued an 1842 model .69-caliber smoothbore that had been rifled or a .54-caliber rifle of the 1817 pattern, perhaps one of the Hall breechloaders made in the 1840s. Few soldiers received the popular "Mississippi" rifle, a handy short-barreled weap-

on, and fewer still got a Model 1855 Springfield rifle musket or an imported British Enfield rifle.

In some regions, military weapons were in such short supply that local authorities called for donations of hunting rifles and shotguns. These were converted in small machine shops for service use. Rifles were cut to uniform length, rebored to .58 caliber and provided with bayonet attachments. Shotguns, with their limited range, were sent to arm cavalry regiments.

More than a year passed before the supply of up-to-date firearms met the demands of the Western armies. All the while, officers grappled with an associated problem—supplying ammunition to fit every type of rifle and musket. Ammunition shortages and mix-ups were so acute at Shiloh that after the battle General Grant ordered his men to swap weapons until each regiment carried arms of the same type.

U.S. MODEL 1822 MUSKET, .69 CALIBER
Altered to percussion between 1843 and 1861, this weapon was the one most widely available to both sides early in the War. It was 57 inches long and weighed slightly more than 10 pounds.

HALL'S BREECHLOADING CARBINE
The Hall carbine, made as a flintlock in 1837 and later converted to percussion, was opened for loading by pressing the lever in front of the trigger. This released the breechblock, which swiveled up to expose the bore. The ramrod doubled as a bayonet when reversed.

U.S. MODEL 1841 "MISSISSIPPI" RIFLE
This rifle was made famous by Jefferson Davis' Mississippi Regiment during the Mexican War. Originally manufactured in .54 caliber, it was rebored to .58. The muzzle of the weapon pictured here was trimmed down on a lathe to accept a socket bayonet.

erate commander in the West, General Albert Sidney Johnston: "He had no army."

Johnston was fortunate in that the Confederates had appointed a single chief for the entire Western front. And to all appearances the Confederacy was fortunate to have Johnston to fill the post. He was the South's beau ideal of a soldier, a man who exuded command presence. He was 58, tall, handsome and stalwart. He had an open face and manner, intelligence and a kindly character that his contemporaries considered noble. In any situation, he could be counted on to take charge with assurance and courage and to inspire men to follow him. He had been two years ahead of Jefferson Davis at West Point and had treated Davis with such kindly authority that the future Confederate President contracted a permanent case of hero worship. Davis considered Johnston the greatest man then living, North or South.

Nor was this just a Southern view. William Tecumseh Sherman described Johnston as "a real general," and Grant said that officers who knew him "expected him to prove the most formidable man that the Confederacy would produce." Old General Winfield Scott, who described Johnston as "a godsend to the Army," offered him high command. When Johnston went to the Confederacy, Federal officers mourned and Confederates celebrated a victory.

This extravagant outpouring of respect and admiration was hardly warranted by Johnston's accomplishments. He had graduated from West Point with a good but unexceptional record in 1826. He served creditably in the Black Hawk War but grew despondent and resigned in 1834 when his young wife was dying of tuberculosis. He went to Texas, arriving just as the revolution ended. Sam Houston made him a general in the Texas Army, but a dueling wound forced him to resign. Johnston was named Secretary of War in a Texas administration that quickly discredited itself. He retired from public life and bought a plantation near Galveston that could not be made to pay.

Johnston was a soldier, not a planter, and he longed to return to uniform. During the Mexican War he organized a Texas regiment, but it reached Zachary Taylor's army after the first battle was finished and disbanded before the next one began. Johnston lingered as a staff officer, then returned to his ruinous plantation. There he struggled, impoverished and increasingly careworn, until the place had to be sold at auction, leaving him heavily in debt. His hopes rose when Taylor became President, but the best he could get was an appointment as an Army paymaster with the rank of major.

Yet none of these setbacks seemed to diminish his nobility of nature or his command presence, and finally his luck turned. In 1855 Jefferson Davis was Secretary of War, and he gave Johnston the colonelcy of a newly formed cavalry regiment. Johnston was brevetted to brigadier general and was in command in California when the Civil War began. Like many Southerners, he considered secession a calamity, but his loyalty to Texas never wavered. He resigned his U.S. commission, rode home to a hero's welcome and then hurried on to Richmond.

President Davis was sick in bed when Johnston arrived. Davis is said to have heard the heavy tread below and exclaimed, "That is Sidney Johnston's step. Bring him up." He made the Texan a full general, second on the list only to Adjutant General Samuel Cooper, who was considered too old to be appointed to a field command. "I hoped and expected that I had others who would prove generals," Davis said later, "but I knew I had one, and that was Sidney Johnston."

So, in early September of 1861, just before Grant seized Paducah, Davis gave Johnston the overall command in the West, as Leonidas Polk had recommended.

Johnston decided to keep troops in neutral Kentucky, though Polk's move to Columbus seemed to be pushing Kentucky toward the Union side. The fact of the matter was that he could not afford to withdraw.

The crucial point in Johnston's command was Nashville, Tennessee, one of the largest cities in the South and an important manufacturing and transportation center. Foundries there were making cannon, a mill was producing 400 pounds of gunpowder daily and clothing factories were turning out uniforms. Warehouses were stuffed with food supplies and leather goods. To lose Nashville would be a devastating blow, yet the only position strong enough to defend was at Bowling Green, Kentucky, where the Green and the Barren Rivers formed a natural barrier to a Federal advance from the north. There was nothing between Bowling Green and Nashville to stop an invading army.

Acting quickly to form his line, Johnston sent Brigadier General Simon Bolivar Buckner, a capable West Pointer from Kentucky who happened to be an old friend of Grant's, to occupy Bowling Green with a column of troops. Johnston noted with interest—his strategy was taking shape—that

In a Federal officer's sketch of the Battle of Belmont, General Grant's endangered troops set fire to a captured camp, denying its supplies to the Confederates. Grant's four infantry regiments and two cavalry companies, in danger of being cut off by a large Confederate force from Columbus, barely made it back to their transports in time to escape.

Union forces in Kentucky reacted with panic to this modest move, thinking it was the start of a massive attack on Louisville, which could drive a salient deep into Kentucky.

Bowling Green was the keystone of Johnston's long defense line. On the right he sent a small force under a colorful Nashville editor named Felix Zollicoffer to occupy the Cumberland Gap, high in the tightly folded mountains near the juncture of Kentucky, Virginia and Tennessee. On the left at Columbus he had Polk, who was fortifying the bluffs that dominated the Mississippi. Johnston's command actually extended through Arkansas, where Brigadier General Ben McCulloch stood guard with his small army, but it already was evident that Federal pressure would come along the Tennessee border.

With these moves, Johnston covered what he saw as the logical attack points. But in addition there were those two fishhook rivers that curved through the South like broad avenues inviting invasion. The Tennessee rose in the eastern part of the state, dipped into Alabama, then turned north through Tennessee to cross the Kentucky line west of Bowling Green and go on to join the Ohio at Paducah. The Cumberland rose in eastern Kentucky, swept down into Tennessee to Nashville, then swung north to run alongside the Tennessee to the Ohio. A fort had been started on each river near the Kentucky line, and Johnston immediately sent engineers to report on the progress of the work.

In Johnston's first speech at Nashville, he addressed the crowd as "fellow soldiers." It was not idle flattery—he needed many more troops to cover his 430-mile line protecting Tennessee. He had fewer than 20,000 ill-armed men on duty—4,000 with Zollicoffer, 4,000 with Buckner and 11,000 with Polk. The Federal forces opposing him numbered 37,000 and were growing rapidly.

An even more pressing problem was his shortage of arms. Almost half of his men were without firearms of any sort; many of those with weapons carried shotguns or hunting rifles. In summary, Johnston protested to Jefferson Davis, "We have not over half the *armed* forces that are now likely to be required." But the President eventually dismissed an envoy from Johnston with a despairing message: "Tell my friend General Johnston that I can do nothing for him, that he must rely on his own resources."

The general's strategy followed naturally from the Federals' obvious concern that his tactical move on Bowling Green was the start of a great invasion: He would run a huge bluff to buy time for building an army. Suddenly Confederate cavalry patrols were doubled and tripled, riding in every direction, striking isolated Union recruiting and training camps. A post at Barboursville, Kentucky, was destroyed. Confederates occupied Albany, Kentucky, for several days, then vanished before a Federal counterattack. Confederate raiders destroyed the lock at the mouth of the Muddy River and occupied Hopkinsville, Kentucky. Regiments marched here, there, back again.

All this activity suggested that Johnston had plenty of men. Soon Southerners themselves began to believe that all was well—the peril of a successful bluff. On the Federal side, Sherman, then at Louisville, put his sanity at question among certain superiors when he told them that he needed 200,000 troops to deal with Johnston's hordes.

In fact Johnston's recruitment campaign was going slowly. Believing that Kentucky's real sympathies lay southward, he expected

Albert Sidney Johnston, portrayed in 1860 wearing his U.S. Army uniform, became the Confederacy's oldest active general at the age of 58. He was a man of heroic physique and high reputation. But his opponent, Ulysses S. Grant, called him "vacillating and undecided in his action."

of holding the left. If those officers were to be heeded, Johnston had nothing to worry about but the center.

The main trouble with that diagnosis was Felix Zollicoffer; he had neither training nor talent in military matters, and his confidence was woefully misplaced. Facing him in eastern Kentucky with an army larger than his was an able West Pointer named George H. Thomas, who would go on to a brilliant career. Zollicoffer maneuvered himself into an indefensible position north of the flooded Cumberland River and then learned, early in 1862, that Thomas intended to attack him.

Zollicoffer could not retreat, so his recently appointed superior, Major General George B. Crittenden, made the decision to attack. On January 19, 1862, after marching all night through rain and shin-deep mud, Zollicoffer's 4,000 exhausted Confederate soldiers clashed with an equal number of Federals on the north bank of the Cumberland in a medium-sized battle dignified by at least five different names, most notably Logan's Cross Roads and Mill Springs. The fighting raged back and forth under a violent storm, but the Federals' solid position and well-rested condition gave them the advantage.

Zollicoffer, conspicuous in his white raincoat, led his first brigade in an attack that drove the Federal cavalry back. But then the battle took an unexpected turn. During fighting at close quarters, Zollicoffer approached an officer and began giving him orders. Zollicoffer happened to be nearsighted and the officer he faced was a Federal colonel, who shot him dead.

Zollicoffer's men, who idolized him, saw him fall and were thrown into confusion. General Crittenden rallied the troops and renewed the assault.

Kentuckians to flock to the Confederate banner, but they were joining at only about half the rate at which the Federal armies were growing. Johnston also issued a call for 30,000 men from Tennessee and 10,000 each from Arkansas and Mississippi. Those states were slow to fill their quotas and Johnston reluctantly lowered his enlistment term from the duration of the War to 12 months.

Johnston's position did not appear to be as bad as it really was. General Zollicoffer was confident of holding Johnston's mountainous right, and Polk was equally confident

At first, the Confederates regained some lost ground, especially in the center, where their fire raked the Federals at close range from a deep ravine. But many of Crittenden's men were armed with old flintlock muskets that failed to fire as their priming powder got wet in the driving rain. In frustration these Confederates smashed their weapons against fence posts, then retreated. Comrades armed with rifles, which used percussion caps rather than loose powder, rushed forward to take their place.

After three hours of desperate fighting, Federal troops of the 9th Ohio mounted a strong bayonet charge. The assault smashed Crittenden's left flank and buckled the entire Confederate line. A Federal officer reported: "The enemy began to waver and give back before the shower of lead and glittering steel brought to bear on his shattered ranks, and he commenced a precipitate retreat under a storm of bullets from our advancing forces until his retreat became a perfect rout."

Crittenden's disorganized troops managed to escape across the rain-swollen Cumberland River on a small steamboat and some barges. But they were forced to leave behind their artillery, tents, mules, much of their food and most of their wounded. They had suffered 500-odd casualties, twice as many as the Federals. Johnston's defense line now lay wide open on the right. However, the mountain terrain was so rough that Thomas was not able to pursue his advantage at once.

By then the War was closing in on Johnston himself. His bluff to win time had succeeded longer than he could have expected, and a real Federal attack was now in the making. It would come, as he had anticipated, up the Tennessee and the Cumberland. Those riv-

ers, curving through his lines, were still his greatest weakness. Unaccountably, the construction of forts defending both rivers had lagged miserably, though everyone realized their importance.

Months before, Governor Isham G. Harris of Tennessee had sent a West Pointer, Brigadier General Daniel S. Donelson, to plan the defense of the two rivers. Donelson, denied

Resplendent in bearskin shakos, the Buckner Guards bivouac at the Louisville Fair Ground in August 1860. They were part of a force of 5,000 militiamen trained and commanded by Simon Bolivar Buckner (inset). Many of the men left neutral Kentucky with him to fight for the Confederacy at the start of hostilities.

the use of better sites within Kentucky because of that state's neutrality, concluded that the most practical place to fortify the Cumberland was on high bluffs a few miles south of the Kentucky border. The Tennessee River was more difficult. He found no truly good defensive position but eventually chose a bend that was only 12 miles from the site for the Cumberland fort.

Engineering studies began and soon the works were started. The fort on the Cumberland was named for Donelson, and the one on the Tennessee was named Fort Henry, supposedly for Confederate Senator Gustavus Henry. Construction went slowly that summer, and by the time General Johnston arrived, neither fort was far enough advanced to provide any real protection against Federal gunboats.

Johnston's military engineers examined the ground and reported that Fort Henry was badly sited. The fort was so low that an ordinary spring rise would put much of it under several feet of water. And across the river were commanding heights from which an enemy could drop plunging fire into the fort. To remove this threat, Johnston ordered men to fortify and hold the high ground. But the only real remedy for Fort Henry was to abandon it and start over at some other point, and there was simply no time for that.

Johnston wanted a strong officer with an engineering background to whip both forts into shape and he nominated Major Alexander P. Stewart, who ultimately would make a name as a Confederate general. But Richmond rejected Stewart and gave the command to Kentuckian Lloyd Tilghman, a West Point-trained brigadier general who had been a practicing civil engineer. Tilghman was appalled when he saw Fort Henry. He bemoaned "its wretched military position" and later declared, underlining the opinion with hard slashes of his pen, *"The history of military engineering records no parallel to this case."*

The indignant general also turned out to be indecisive and dilatory. He called for 1,000 plantation slaves to carry forward the

Federal Colonel Speed S. Fry shoots and kills Confederate Brigadier General Felix Zollicoffer in an imaginative engraving of the close-range fighting at Mill Springs, Kentucky. One of Zollicoffer's officers, at right, warns him too late, "It's the enemy, General!"

work. Only about 500 slaves arrived, and then Tilghman could not decide how to use them or whether it was really worthwhile to continue construction. Inexplicably Johnston left the defense of his most vulnerable point in the shaky hands of an officer whom he had not wanted in the first place.

Late in January, Johnston's force in Tennessee and Kentucky had grown to perhaps 45,000 all told—and he knew he was facing at least twice that many Federal soldiers. By the time news came of Zollicoffer's disaster in the East, Federal gunboats were probing up the Tennessee, and Johnston learned that Tilghman had hardly started the works on the heights across from Fort Henry. "It is most extraordinary!" Johnston snapped. He had ordered those works months before, "and now, with the enemy upon us, nothing

has been done." He telegraphed Tilghman: OCCUPY AND INTRENCH THE HEIGHTS OPPOSITE FORT HENRY. DO NOT LOSE A MOMENT. WORK ALL NIGHT.

On the Union side, meanwhile, the unfortunate General Frémont had departed on November 2, setting off wholesale changes in command structure. Frémont's Western Department had been split in two: the Department of Kansas, which went to Major General David Hunter, and the Department of Missouri, a huge territory stretching from Arkansas and western Kentucky to Minnesota and Wisconsin, which was assigned to Major General Henry Wager Halleck. Brigadier General Don Carlos Buell replaced Sherman as commander of the Department of the Ohio, which included Kentucky east of the Cumberland and Tennessee; Sherman's alarm at General Johnston's bluff had grown so great as to amount to a nervous breakdown. Both Halleck and Buell argued that the splitting of Frémont's command was a clumsy and even dangerous arrangement, and each man wanted it to be put back together, with himself at its head.

Halleck, taking over in St. Louis, was a strange, difficult man, much respected and much disliked. His reputation as a military theoretician prompted Army men to nickname him Old Brains. But he offended many with his arrogant and unabashedly self-seeking manner; he devoted much effort to the twin goals of expanding his command and making sure that no blame of any sort fell on him. Yet he was an excellent administrator—perhaps the War's best—and a skillful manager of the Army's relations with the politicians and the press.

Halleck and Buell were highly impressed with the showy demonstrations that Sidney Johnston was making along his Tennessee line and had no inclination to chance a serious engagement. This timidity was disconcerting in the extreme to President Lincoln, who through a long, discontented winter of inactivity was ever more urgently demanding action. He expected Halleck and Buell to act in concert, which neither was willing to do; both wished to continue building, arming and training their separate forces. Meanwhile, the original idea of advancing down the Mississippi had been rendered impractical by the 140 guns that Leonidas Polk had dug into the bluffs of Columbus. Taking the place by assault, Halleck told McClellan, would mean "an immense siege train and a terrible loss of life." Instead, Halleck's attention was more and more drawn to the same weakness that Johnston had perceived: the riverine avenues of invasion provided by the Cumberland and Tennessee.

What made these routes more attractive was the recent growth of the fresh-water navy into an important military force. The river gunboat fleet (*pages 68-77*) had started out with three steamboats that had been converted into gunboats and protected with thick oak slabs to withstand small-arms fire. These ships proved themselves immediately. They made reconnaissance runs, provided most of the limited information commanders received and supported troop movements by river, including the unscathed withdrawal of Grant's crowded troopships after the Battle of Belmont. Wherever the gunboats went, they inspired awe.

But woodclad gunboats would be shot to kindling by heavy guns like those at Columbus—or even Fort Henry. The answer was ironclad boats designed from scratch to fight shore batteries. A St. Louis riverman and salvage expert named James B. Eads was put to work urgently to produce new boats.

The ironclad concept was new, and although marine architects and engine specialists were drawn in, no one was sure of what to do. Eads wound up using his river-bred ingenuity freely. What finally slid down Eads's ways were seven marvelous gunboats named after Western river ports: *St. Louis, Carondelet, Louisville, Pittsburgh, Mound City, Cincinnati* and *Cairo*.

Their appearance, with everything hidden behind iron except their smokestacks, was stunning—and perhaps a bit comical: "They looked like enormous turtles," said newspaperman Albert Richardson. Eads also converted two steamboats—the *Benton* and the *Essex*—into ironclad gunboats.

Professional naval officers ran all these boats. The crews were a mixture of salt-water men from the East, fresh-water sailors from the Great Lakes, rivermen and—as Henry Walke, commander of the *Carondelet*, put it—"just enough men-o'-war's men to leaven the lump with naval discipline."

The final ingredient that made the gunboats potent weapons was the arrival of a commander who, like Grant, believed that the way to deal with the enemy was to attack him forthwith. Andrew Hull Foote reached the West as a salt-water captain and was soon designated a flag officer, equivalent to a general in a period when the Navy was not using the grade of admiral. He had a blunt, implacable resolve; when angered he was "savage and demoniacal," James Eads said. Foote had experienced a shipboard conversion to militant Christianity; thereafter he crusaded passionately against the issuance of grog to sailors, made the U.S.S. *Cumberland* the first temperance ship in the Navy and regularly preached Sunday sermons to his men.

Foote's fierce intensity sometimes racked him with sick headaches. Yet he was amiable except when angry, and Captain Walke said "there was a sailor-like heartiness and frankness about him that made his company very desirable." After a lifetime on blue water under a cloud of sail, Foote did not consider armored monsters on a muddy river ideal, but he grew enthusiastic about the fighting qualities of his strange craft and became eager to attack. The gunboats were based at Cairo, the controlling spot on the rivers, and Foote and Grant were much together.

Grant had seen his army at Cairo grow to more than 20,000 men by January; he was spoiling to use them, and Fort Henry seemed to be a likely target. Grant's interest in that position was soon confirmed by the commander of his troops at Paducah, Brigadier General Charles F. Smith. This tough old Regular Army officer had been commandant of cadets at West Point when Grant was a cadet there. At the time, Grant had regarded Smith and General Scott as the two men most to be envied in all the world. Grant was still inordinately respectful of Smith and had trouble giving him orders. But Smith, a professional to the core, soon put him at ease.

In January, while Grant's men were out on a demonstration, General Smith took the gunboat *Lexington* up the Tennessee River and looked over Fort Henry. It enclosed about three acres of ground in a five-sided earthwork parapet eight feet high. Confederate gunners fired at him, but ineffectively. On his return Smith wrote Grant, "I think two ironclad gunboats would make short work of Fort Henry."

Smith's opinion convinced Grant that an attack on Fort Henry would succeed. To make a case for the assault, Grant went to St. Louis to talk to his arrogant superior, General Halleck. But he had hardly started speaking when Halleck cut him off. Halleck had been considering such a move for weeks, and he wanted no advice from a junior officer. That exchange keynoted the difficult relationship between Grant and Halleck. Grant wrote, "I returned to Cairo very much crestfallen."

Grant continued to press for an attack. A few days later he wired Halleck: WITH PERMISSION, I WILL TAKE FORT HENRY, ON THE TENNESSEE, AND ESTABLISH AND HOLD A LARGE CAMP THERE. Foote also wired Halleck, saying that he and Grant could take Fort Henry, and prodding

Major General Henry Wager Halleck, the abrasive commander of the Federal Department of the Missouri, was in the habit of scratching his elbows while thinking. It was as if—said Secretary of the Navy Gideon Welles, who detested him—Halleck's elbows were the seat of his mental process.

Halleck with a direct request: HAVE WE YOUR AUTHORITY TO MOVE FOR THAT PURPOSE WHEN READY?

By now Halleck also had received Smith's appraisal and was inclined to agree; he put much stock in Smith. But what may actually have forced his decision was a message from Washington that the fabulous Confederate General Pierre Gustave Toutant Beauregard, the man who had reduced Fort Sumter and routed the Union Army at Bull Run, was heading west, allegedly with 15 regiments, to support Sidney Johnston. Halleck wired Grant: MAKE YOUR PREPARATIONS TO TAKE AND HOLD FORT HENRY.

On February 2, 1862, Grant loaded 17,000 men on steamboats and started up the Tennessee with seven of Foote's gunboats in escort. On the afternoon of February 3, the boats paused several miles below Fort Henry. Grant wanted to land his men just beyond the range of the fort's guns, and to find out their range he steamed upstream in the *Essex* and opened fire.

Inside the fort, the artillery chief, Captain Jesse Taylor, answered with one of his best cannon, a 6-inch rifle. Its crew put a shot into the *Essex* that rattled about without doing much harm. The Confederate gunners cheered as the *Essex* fell quickly downstream. But Grant had his answer. Soon he began landing his men.

In the meantime, Fort Henry's strongest enemy—the river itself—was coming up swiftly. Downstream on the *Carondelet*, Captain Walke noted that "the swift current brought down an immense quantity of heavy driftwood, lumber, fences and large trees, and it required all the steam-power with both anchors down to prevent the boat from being dragged."

At first General Tilghman was not dismayed by the approach of the gunboats; in a wire to Sidney Johnston, he said that if reinforced quickly he had A GLORIOUS CHANCE TO OVERWHELM THE ENEMY. But no reinforcements were forthcoming, and the water crept inside the gates of the fort and kept rising.

By the morning of February 5, the water was two feet deep at General Tilghman's flagpole. Soon his guns at the lowest level would be flooded. And he did not like the looks of the great flotilla of troop transports that was following the gunboats. "Far as the eye could see," wrote artillerist Taylor, "the course of the river could be traced by the dense volumes of smoke issuing from the flotilla." So Tilghman finally realized that there would be no possibility of saving the fort. He decided to pull out the bulk of his men and send them 12 miles to safety at Fort Donelson.

Taylor wrote that the general "turned to me with the question, 'Can you hold out for one hour against a determined attack?' I replied that I could." Taylor kept 54 infantrymen and part of an artillery company, and Tilghman led 2,500 troops away. When the main garrison was well on the road to Fort Donelson, Tilghman and some of his staff turned back to fight with Taylor's sacrificial company.

On the morning of February 6, Grant's troops set out on both sides of the river. A

In a patriotic lithograph of 1862, Flag Officer Andrew H. Foote plants his feet firmly on the deck of a gunboat, with other ironclads backing him up. A devout Presbyterian, Foote often gathered his crews on deck and preached fire-and-brimstone sermons.

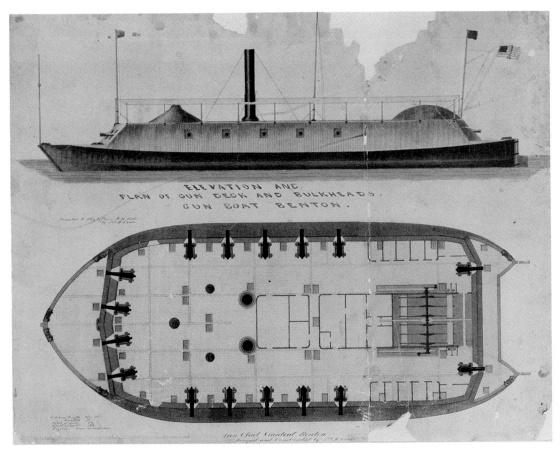

ELEVATION AND
PLAN OF GUN DECK AND BULKHEADS.
GUN BOAT BENTON.

The U.S.S. *Benton* was the largest and most powerful vessel of the Federal river fleet. These drawings were made for her conversion from a snag boat to an ironclad mounting 16 cannon.

Foote opened fire at 1,700 yards from his flagship, the *Cincinnati*, giving the signal for general firing. On the *Essex*, Second Mate James Laning had instructions to hold fire until he saw the effect of the *Cincinnati's* shots. "The first three shots from the flagship fell short, so there was $24 worth of ammunition expended," he said. He increased elevation and cut loose with a ferocious roar. "The fort seemed a blaze of fire, whilst the boom of the cannon's roar was almost deafening. The wind was blowing across our bows, carrying the smoke away rapidly. Our fleet kept slowly approaching the fort and gradually shortening the distance. Our shells, which were fused at 15 seconds, were reduced to ten, and then to five seconds. The elevation of the guns was depressed from seven degrees to six, five and four and then three degrees, and every shot went straight home, none from the *Essex* falling short."

The gunboat attack had been timed to coincide with the arrival of the infantry, but the men had encountered deep mud and were far behind schedule. The troops heard the fire of the gunboats. Captain John Rector remembered, "We knew that the engagement had commenced, but by that time we were behind a tree-capped hill and our view of the scene was cut off. Soon the roar of the guns was almost continuous and we could see from the smoke that rose in dense clouds that the fleet was gradually getting nearer to the fort. The excitement in our ranks was intense."

Inside the fort, Taylor and his men were waiting. He had assigned each gun a specific boat as target. As the boats approached, they "increased the rapidity of their fire, until they showed one broad and leaping sheet of

column under General Smith moved to seize the heights opposite the fort, and one under Brigadier General John A. McClernand advanced to cut the garrison's escape route. The gunboats would sail up and attack the fort head on. Foote visited the boats to offer a ringing prayer and firm instructions. Aboard the *Essex* he said, "Be sure you do not throw any ammunition away. Every charge you fire costs the government about eight dollars. If your shots fall short you encourage the enemy. If they reach home you demoralize him and get the worth of your money."

flame.'' When the gunboats were a mile away, the fort commenced firing in "as pretty and simultaneous a broadside as I ever saw flash from the sides of a frigate.'' By now several of his 17 guns were underwater, but Taylor's skeleton crews kept the others going. This exchange continued as the boats drew steadily forward, finally closing to 300 yards, point-blank range.

Then the fort's two most important guns were disabled. The big 6-inch rifle burst with a roar, disabling its crew. A little later the big 128-pounder somehow fouled itself and could not be fired without lengthy repairs. The only weapons that had been really effective against the gunboats were silent. Not long after that, Taylor wrote, "two of the 32-pounders were struck almost at the same instant, and the flying fragments of the shattered guns and bursted shells disabled every man at the two guns. Rifle shot and shell penetrated the earthworks as readily as a ball from a navy Colt would pierce a pine board, and soon so disabled other guns as to leave us but four capable of being served.''

The Federal gunboat flotilla attacks Fort Henry four abreast on February 6, 1862. As the flagship *Cincinnati* (*left*), the *Carondelet* and the *St. Louis* shell the fort, the *Essex* is hit in the boiler and put out of action.

Yet the fort also was making itself felt. Captain Walke was watching Foote's flag steamer "when one of the enemy's heavy shot struck her. It had the effect, apparently, of a thunderbolt, ripping her side timbers and scattering the splinters over the vessel. She did not slacken her speed, but moved on as though nothing unexpected had happened." The *Cincinnati* took 31 hits, suffering most of the damage in unarmored areas. "Her chimneys, after-cabin and boats were completely riddled," Walke said. "Two of her guns were disabled. One was struck by a 68-pounder on the muzzle. A 32-pounder shot struck on her side, and dented the iron. The only fatal shot from the fort passed through just at the larboard front, killing one man instantly, carrying his head away."

The real carnage was on the unfortunate *Essex*. She took 14 shots before one crashed through the port casemate and burst her center boiler. This shot, wrote James Laning, opened "a chasm for the escape of scald-ing steam and water. The scene that followed was almost indescribable." Laning, who happened to be away from the blast area, was met by a crowd of men rushing aft. He looked out the stern port and saw men in the water. "The steam and hot water in the forward gun-deck had driven all who were able to get out of the ports overboard, except a few who were fortunate enough to cling to the casemate outside."

The commander of the *Essex*, Captain John Porter, was scalded by a direct blast of steam and threw himself blindly from a port. As he went into the water, a seaman caught him about the waist and held him until another sailor could lift him onto the narrow platform outside the casemate.

Laning continued: "In a very few minutes our gallant ship was drifting slowly away; her commander badly wounded, a number of her officers and crew dead at their posts, whilst many others were writhing in their last agony. As soon as the scalding steam would admit, the forward gun-deck was explored. The pilots, who were both in the pilot-house, were scalded to death. A seaman named James Coffey, who was shot-man to the No. 2 gun, was on his knees in the act of taking a shell from the box to be passed to the loader. The escaping steam had struck him square in the face and he met death in that position. Theo P. Terry was severely scalded and died in a few days. Our loss in killed, wounded and missing amounted to 32."

From the fort, artillery Captain Taylor observed, "When the *Essex* dropped out of the fight I could see her men wildly throwing themselves into the swollen river." But the fort's situation was desperate, too. Only four guns were still firing, the men were exhaust-

Brigadier General Lloyd Tilghman, in command at Fort Henry, fought valiantly before giving up. When he came aboard the *Cincinnati* to surrender, Flag Officer Foote said, "Come, general, you have lost your dinner, and the steward has just told me that mine is ready." They walked together into the cabin.

A 6-inch gun in Fort Henry bursts during the Federal gunboat attack, killing a sergeant and wounding the rest of the crew. After 70 minutes of bombardment, only four of the fort's 17 guns were still in action.

ed and further fighting seemed futile. "We had been required to hold for an hour," Taylor wrote proudly, and "we had held out for over two."

General Tilghman, who had returned to the fort during the attack, told Taylor it was time to surrender. They now saw that the flagpole had been hit by cannon fire and the halyards fouled. Taylor called for a sergeant who had served aboard a man-of-war, "and we ran across to the flag staff and up the lower rigging to the cross-trees, and succeeded in clearing the halyards and lowering the flag." The gunboats, he said, "now apparently within 200 yards of the fort, were in perfect security, and with the coolness and precision of target practice were sweeping the entire fort."

Marching at quick time in hopes of getting in on the action, Captain Rector was still far from Fort Henry when he and his men heard the firing stop. On the *Essex*, Laning told Captain Porter that they were victorious. "He immediately rallied, and, raising himself on his elbow, called for three cheers, and gave two himself, falling exhausted on the mattress in his effort to give the third." When the flag went down, the *Cincinnati* lowered a launch, which rowed through the flooded fort's main gate and past cannon that were now underwater. Tilghman went out to the *Cincinnati* and surrendered formally to Foote.

That afternoon Grant wired Halleck, and Halleck wired Washington, the same message: FORT HENRY IS OURS. The meaning of the message was entirely clear: Albert Sidney Johnston's Tennessee line had been breached, and the war in the West was starting to move.

The Federal river fleet lies at anchor on the Ohio River near the Mound City naval station, five miles north of Cairo, Illinois. The *St. Louis (center)* was the first of Eads's seven nearly identical ironclads. To distinguish the boats, different-colored bands were painted on their smokestacks.

Building a Federal Riverboat Fleet

Federal planners, judging correctly that the war in the West might well hinge on control of the region's rivers, decided by May of 1861 to build a fleet of warships that would be specially adapted to navigating those tricky rivers. The man who won the contract to produce these ships was the ideal choice. James B. Eads was a veteran riverman, a salvage expert and an imaginative, hard-driving taskmaster. He was also a millionaire and could afford to advance large sums of money when Federal funding was slow.

Eads and his associates faced problems of enormous technical difficulty. Their ships had to be strongly protected to withstand bombardment from the Confederate forts that were scattered along the banks of the rivers. The vessels had to mount cannon as heavy as the fixed Confederate artillery. Yet despite the great weight of their guns and protective gear, they had to be so shallow of draft that they could navigate in less than 10 feet of water.

While a naval officer from Washington completed the first makeshift gunboats, Eads's engineers and construction crews went to work and improvised freely. They rebuilt two paddle-wheelers and encased them in iron armor. In the meantime, they began building seven ironclads designed for bombarding Confederate forts.

The final products were not without serious structural flaws. They were slow and hard to maneuver, and their unarmored decks were vulnerable to plunging shot. All the same, the ships were wonderfully successful and thoroughly intimidating. A young seaman on one of the ironclads conceded that their appearance was ludicrous—"of the mud-turtle school of architecture, with just a dash of Pollywog treatment by way of relief." But, he added, "they struck terror into every guilty soul as they floated down the river."

The Timberclads: Three Stopgap Gunboats

The first gunboats to be completed were the work of U.S. Navy Commander John Rodgers, who was sent west in the spring of 1861 to organize a river fleet. Rodgers, anxious to deploy gunboats on the rivers as quickly as possible, purchased three flat-bottomed side-wheelers in Cincinnati, and in June he commissioned their conversion into gunboats. The remodeled vessels were named the *Lexington*, the *Tyler* and the *Conestoga*.

Rodgers had the steamers' upper works stripped away and their frames and decks strengthened with heavy timbers to accommodate the weight of four to eight heavy guns. These cannon—32-pounder smoothbores and 8-inch rifled guns—gave the ships a great edge over any Confederate vessel on the rivers. Finally, Rodgers had the three ships sheathed with oak planks five inches thick.

The timberclads were completed by the end of the summer. Although they could not stand up to heavy cannon fire, the new gunboats proved invaluable in several ways. They reconnoitered and raided Confederate bases well upstream. And they supported such Army operations as General Grant's attack on Belmont.

The *Lexington*, a side-wheeler converted into a timberclad gunboat, took part in the first actions by the Western Flotilla. On August 22, 1861, she captured a Confederate steamer, and on September 4, along with the *Tyler*, she attacked Confederate batteries along the Mississippi.

Wooden Ships Armored in Iron

James Eads used his experience as a salvager to convert two riverboats into ironclad gunboats. The first, a five-year-old ferry, was quickly rebuilt (*right*) and pressed into action as the *Essex*. The second ship—Eads's pride and joy—took much longer.

Eads persuaded Washington to convert a snag boat—a peculiarly Western vessel that was used to raise sunken ships and submerged trees—into a gunboat to take advantage of its great size and stability. By the autumn of 1861 he had begun work on the *Benton*, an enormous catamaran 202 feet long and 72 feet in the beam. The vessel's bow and sides were covered with iron three and a half inches thick and pierced with gunports for 16 cannon. The finished ship, which was crewed by 176 men, was the most effective gunboat in the Western Flotilla, and as steady as a rock.

The ponderous *Benton* moves slowly, driven by two high-pressure engines. When the commander of the Western Flotilla, Flag Officer Foote, complained, a subordinate said she was "plenty fast enough to fight with."

Another ironclad in the making, the ferry *New Era* is bolstered with heavy timber during the first stage of her conversion.

The former *New Era*, her timber reinforcement overlaid with heavy iron plate, emerges as the ironclad *Essex*. A much smaller vessel than the *Benton*, the *Essex* carried five guns and a crew of 124.

The Turtles: Eads's Overnight Wonders

Starting in August of 1861, work crews under the direction of James Eads laid the keels for seven new ironclads, four of them at Carondelet near St. Louis and the rest at Mound City. The vessels, developed from the plans of Naval Constructor Samuel Pook and often called "Pook's Turtles," were built expressly to fight Confederate shore batteries.

Each of the seven ironclads was 175 feet long and 51.2 feet in the beam. The casemate, its walls slanted at about 35 degrees to deflect enemy fire, was protected with iron plate two and a half inches thick on the bow and sides. Each vessel was armed with 13 cannon and was powered by two high-compression steam engines that could propel the ship upstream at five miles per hour and downstream at nine miles per hour.

Eads's construction crews swelled to include 4,000 men and worked at full speed, often by torchlight well into the night. Timber for the vessels came by barge from seven states; machine shops and foundries in St. Louis worked around the clock; Eads paid bonuses to urge the men onward. On October 12, just two months after work began, the *St. Louis* was launched, and the other six ironclads would follow by January 15, 1862. These ships soon proved to be the backbone of the Federal river fleet.

Under construction on the Missouri River, two Eads ironclads standing stern to stern take shape at the Carondelet shipyard near St. Louis. Just below deck level in the foreground are the ship's five boilers.

The most famous of the seven ironclads built by James B. Eads, the U.S.S. *Carondelet* carries four heavy guns on each broadside as well as three forward and two

astern. The *Carondelet* was under fire longer and more often than any other vessel in the Western Flotilla.

Clash at Fort Donelson

"A great shouting was heard behind me, whereupon I sent an orderly to ascertain the cause. The man reported the road and woods full of soldiers apparently in rout. An officer then rode by at full speed, shouting 'All's lost! Save yourselves!'"

BRIGADIER GENERAL LEW WALLACE, U.S. ARMY, FEBRUARY 15, 1862, FORT DONELSON

The day after Fort Henry fell, journalist Albert Richardson of the *New York Tribune* went to see Grant. Richardson had been summoned to his home office and wanted to say good-by.

"You had better wait a day or two," Grant said.

"Why?"

"I am going over to attack Fort Donelson tomorrow."

Richardson was surprised by his casual tone. The fort, 12 miles away on the Cumberland River, was stronger than Fort Henry. All of Henry's garrison except for a few score gunners had retreated there, and surely the Confederates were pouring in reinforcements.

"Do you know how strong it is?" Richardson asked.

"Not exactly," Grant said, "but I think we can take it; at all events, we can try."

That was typical of the man, Richardson observed later: Where there was something to be done, Grant tended to go right ahead and do it. The capture of Fort Henry, resounding victory though it was, had put the Federal army in a dangerously exposed position. Grant could not expect to hold his prize long if he did not take Fort Donelson.

Back in St. Louis, Major General Henry Halleck understood the threat. He feared that the Confederates might march from Fort Donelson across that narrow neck of land and demolish Grant, whom he considered impulsive and careless. Even as Halleck

reinforced Grant for an advance, he sent him entrenching tools and told him to improve his position at Fort Henry so it could be used as a base. But Grant side-stepped the order; Fort Henry was still flooded, and anyway, he was going to Donelson.

He did delay a little, though. Halleck was sending 10,000 more men, and Grant wanted to wait for them to arrive. Even more important, Flag Officer Andrew Foote needed several days to go down the Tennessee River, pause at Cairo for repairs and then take his fleet up the Cumberland to Fort Donelson. In the meantime, the three wooden gunboats under Lieutenant Commander S. L. Phelps made a devastating run up the Tennessee that demonstrated in the most graphic way the extent to which Sidney Johnston's defense line in Tennessee had been breached. The little squadron damaged a vital railroad upriver from Fort Henry, left behind a trail of burned Confederate boats and went as far as Florence, Alabama. There was nothing on the Tennessee or the Cumberland to challenge the squat, ugly vessels.

For General Johnston, the message was obvious: No defense in depth was possible in Tennessee when a Federal army could be landed, supplied and reinforced behind any position he might choose. He told his government, "I think the gunboats of the enemy will probably take Fort Donelson without the necessity of employing their land force in cooperation."

The fact was that Johnston's magnificent

bluff, which had kept some Federal commanders in a state of nervous prostration for five months, had at last been called. Despite the time that he had bought for his side, the Confederates had failed to muster the men and the weapons to defend Tennessee. At this point, Johnston had about 45,000 troops in total. He was opposing better-armed forces of at least twice that number. These included Grant's small advance army, Halleck's men in Missouri and Buell's army in Kentucky, which alone was larger than Johnston's entire force.

With the Federals in Fort Henry forming a deep salient in the Confederate line, Johnston's position at Bowling Green, Kentucky, and Polk's fortified position at Columbus, Kentucky, were separated and could be taken by Grant from the flank or the rear. Johnston decided that his only recourse was to retreat. He would abandon Bowling Green, Columbus and Fort Donelson and move south to positions below the Tennessee River in Alabama. Since he had been holding Bowling Green to defend Nashville, with its important commerce and industry, Johnston's planned withdrawal meant that he was also resigned to abandoning Nashville. Perhaps this retreat would awaken the Confederacy to its true peril and galvanize the great effort needed to raise men and arms.

On February 7, the day after Fort Henry fell, Johnston went to the Covington house, in Bowling Green, to review matters with his newly arrived second-in-command, General Beauregard. The Louisiana Frenchman, a vain, touchy man, had quarreled with President Davis over the conduct of the War, and Davis was only too glad to oblige the Westerners, who demanded action, by sending the prestigious general west. Beauregard was

so dismayed to learn of Johnston's weakness that he was ready to throw it all up and go back to Virginia. But Johnston talked him into staying awhile and gloomily explained his retreat plan.

Beauregard suggested massing the entire army at Fort Donelson: There it would smash Grant, then wheel to deal with the huge Federal army in Kentucky. But Johnston feared that if the plan failed, the Confederate cause in the West would be in a shambles. The retreat would go as planned.

But what should Johnston do about Fort Donelson, where 5,000 men were digging trenches to resist Grant's 17,000? He had two reasonable alternatives. As Beauregard suggested, he could concentrate his troops at Donelson to outnumber and defeat Grant's army. Or he could leave a small sacrifice garrison at Donelson to hold the fort until he withdrew the bulk of his army intact. Johnston chose neither course. Instead, quite inexplicably, he left the 5,000 men in Donelson and gradually committed 12,000 more, totaling 37 per cent of his force—this to defend a place that he thought gunboats alone could destroy. It was as if his mind told him that Donelson was hopeless but his heart told him to fight there.

Then he compounded the problem by his choice of commanders. His troops at Bowling Green were under the immediate command of a competent soldier, Major General William J. Hardee, who had graduated from West Point in Beauregard's class and also had served as the Military Academy's commandant of cadets. Johnston could have left the retreat from Bowling Green in Hardee's hands and gone himself to make the most of a stand at Donelson. Or he could have sent the flashy Beauregard to Donelson.

Turmoil in East Tennessee

While Confederate troops in western Tennessee were bracing to meet the Federal onslaught at Forts Henry and Donelson, Confederate authorities in East Tennessee were fighting for the hearts and minds of their own citizens. Though the state as a whole had voted overwhelmingly to join the Confederacy, its mountainous east remained a bastion of Unionism. The sole exception was Knoxville, the largest city in the eastern area; here the town fathers and two out of three of the local voters favored the Confederacy.

For a while, both sides held recruiting rallies in Knoxville, sometimes on the same street (*below*). But feelings became too strong for peaceful competition. A pro-Union gathering in May 1861 was disrupted by shooting. In time, thousands of Unionists joined guerrilla bands or enlisted in Federal armies.

Confederate officials tried to woo the recalcitrant mountaineers with friendly persuasion and a guaranteed secret ballot in the August elections for the Confederate Congress. The tactics failed embarrassingly: The mountaineers elected Union candidates.

Authorities now had no choice but to crack down. Pro-Union leaders were imprisoned and attempts were made to disarm the citizens. Other Confederates took the law into their own hands, beating, butchering and lynching resisters. The passions inflamed by these episodes led to guerrilla warfare, and would outlast the War itself.

Beneath their respective flags, Union and Confederate recruiters address prospective soldiers at the ends of Gay Street in Knoxville, Tennessee, in 1861.

Instead he ran the Bowling Green retreat himself, sent Beauregard to take charge of the withdrawal of Polk's troops from Columbus and left his men at Donelson under a clumsy triumvirate of brigadiers. The best of these three was Simon Bolivar Buckner, who had quit the Army in 1855, become the manager of his wife's estate in Louisville and returned to fight for the Confederacy as commander of the force that seized Bowling Green. Though Buckner was the ablest, he was third in rank among the three and was given little voice in what followed. Higher in authority was Gideon J. Pillow, a self-important lawyer and politician from Tennessee who felt that a command in the Mexican War and a couple of minor wounds made him a premier soldier. Pillow was the only Confederate commander whom Grant held in open contempt.

Over these uninspiring figures was a thoroughly discouraging one: John B. Floyd, formerly Governor of Virginia and Secretary of War under President Buchanan. A politician hopelessly out of his depth in a war, Floyd lacked both training and talent in military affairs—shortages made worse by his vacillating nature. Before coming west, he had served just long enough in western Virginia to demonstrate his incompetence with stunning clarity.

The Confederate brigadiers established their headquarters in a comfortable inn in Dover, Tennessee, a little south of Donelson, and presided with interest over construction to strengthen the fort's ambitious defenses against land assault. The defense line was a semicircle of earthworks enclosing both the fort and the town; its southern end curved back almost to the river, and its unfinished northern section was protected by deep swamps along a flooded creek. The river approach was protected by two formidable batteries set high on a bluff. General Pillow liked the fort's chances far better than Johnston did. I WILL NEVER SURRENDER THE POSITION, he telegraphed, AND WITH GOD'S HELP I MEAN TO MAINTAIN IT.

On February 12, Grant and 15,000 of his troops made the 12-mile march from Henry to Donelson. The weather was mild, and the lighthearted Illinois and Iowa men, deciding that spring had come, discarded their blankets and overcoats along the roads. Only a spattering of shots from roving Confederate cavalry disturbed the march. "We kept closing in slowly," said Lieutenant W. D. Harland of the 18th Illinois, "and at dusk were within pistol shot of their rifle pits."

Grant had set up his headquarters in the kitchen of a nearby farmhouse, taking over a feather bed near the fireplace. In the morning, he moved to complete the investment, placing the division of General Smith, his old idol, on the left and sending out to the right Brigadier General John A. McClernand, an energetic but inexperienced political appointee from Illinois. Though McClernand's division was stretched thin, it did not reach the river on the right, which left the Confederates an escape route. Grant was anxious to close the gap. He was expecting to put the troops Halleck had sent in the center, moving McClernand's division farther to the right to close the exit. Since the reinforcements had not arrived, Grant summoned Brigadier General Lew Wallace (later the author of *Ben Hur* and other popular novels) from Fort Henry with 2,000 men—practically all the rest of Grant's army.

Late that afternoon the wind shifted to

the north and a cold drizzle began. At dark the drizzle turned to sleet. The temperature fell to 10° F. "Guns, caissons and wagons were frozen in the earth," Albert Richardson wrote. Men who had abandoned coats and blankets now were in agony. There were no tents. Sharpshooters were active on both sides and to light a fire at night was to invite a bullet. For food there was only hardtack, and without fires there was no coffee. For many soldiers on both sides this was the worst night in the War. "Suffered severely," Lieutenant Harland noted in his diary. Young Wilbur F. Crummer of the 45th Illinois crawled under a pile of leaves, found they gave him no warmth and paced away the night.

General McClernand had added substantially to his men's misery. On the 13th he had sent three regiments on an unauthorized attack against bothersome Confederate guns on a fortified hill. The assault was beaten back with heavy casualties. Some of the wounded were burned to death when cannon fire ignited leaves and grass. Wounded men who escaped the flames lay in the cold, slowly freezing to death. By morning, said an Illinois brigade commander, most of his men "were nearly torpid."

That morning, the 14th, Flag Officer Andrew Foote's gunboat flotilla and 12 Army transports with 10,000 troops from Halleck arrived and tied up three miles below Fort Donelson. General Wallace and the troops from Fort Henry also arrived, and most of the new men were formed in a third division under Wallace. Grant asked Foote to attack the fort immediately. Foote agreed with reluctance; he had only the meager reconnaissance provided by Captain Henry Walke, who had arrived early on the *Carondelet* and

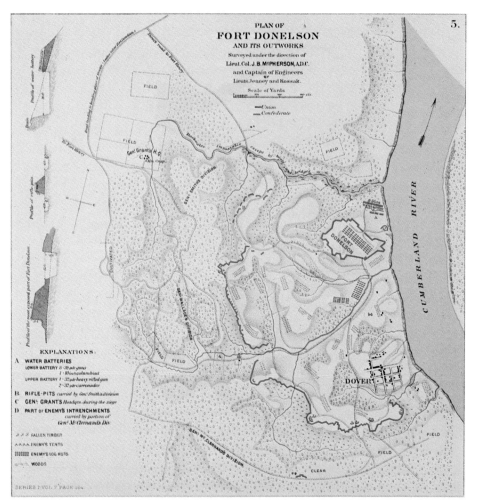

had gone up to Donelson the day before to trade shots.

Grant's plan was a simple one. He expected the boats to destroy the fort's two waterside batteries; then they would move above the fort, threatening the road south over which the Confederates might escape and bombarding their trenches from the rear.

Foote spent the morning getting the boats ready, piling their upper decks with chains, lumber and bags of coal to protect them from plunging fire. It was 3 p.m. before the ironclads came up the river in battle line: the *Louisville* to the west; then Foote's flag

This U.S. Army map shows the initial deployment of Federal and Confederate forces at Fort Donelson. The Confederates tried to break out through General McClernand's division on February 15, 1862, but General Lew Wallace's division moved south to seal off the escape corridor and General Smith's division stormed the Confederates' right flank.

steamer, the *St. Louis;* then the *Pittsburgh* and the *Carondelet;* and two wooden gunboats. When the *Louisville* and the *Pittsburgh* fell back, Foote popped out of his pilothouse with a megaphone and bellowed, "Steam up!" The pugnacious Walke went ahead of the flagship and was also reprimanded by megaphone.

At 3:30 p.m., at a range of less than 2,000 yards, the *St. Louis* opened fire. The gunners in Fort Donelson's batteries did not respond; they wanted the gunboats closer. Shells exploded against the thick earthworks before them, throwing up geysers of dirt. General Floyd decided that his fort would not last 20 minutes. A tough amateur cavalryman named Nathan Bedford Forrest, who rapidly was making himself a professional soldier, watched the bombardment in anguish. He turned to his aide, who had been a preacher in private life, and cried, "Parson, for God's sake pray! Nothing but God Almighty can save that fort!"

As the boats closed to about 1,000 yards, the fort opened fire with its biggest guns, a 10-inch smoothbore Columbiad and a 32-pounder rifled gun. The boats came on until they were within 400 yards and at that range all the 12 Confederate guns facing the river could reach them. The Confederates were using mostly solid shot, hoping to penetrate armor. And they knew that they were hitting—the river rang like a great forge, iron striking iron. Foote's lack of enthusiasm for the attack was proving fully justified.

Said Walke of the *Carondelet:* "Soon a 128-pounder struck our anchor, smashed it into flying bolts, and bounded over the vessel, taking away a part of our smoke stack. Another ripped up the iron plating and glanced over; another went through the plating and lodged in the heavy casemate; another struck the pilothouse, knocked the plating to pieces, and sent fragments of iron and splinters into the pilots, one of whom fell mortally wounded; and still they came, harder and faster, taking flagstaffs and smoke stacks and tearing off the side armor as lightning tears the bark from a tree."

In the waterside batteries the Confederates were taking heart; they could see the damage they were doing. "Now, boys,"

A Federal soldier wounded in General McClernand's unauthorized attack on an outpost at Fort Donelson burns to death in a brush fire started by gunfire on the bitter-cold night of February 13, 1862. Many wounded men on both sides were incinerated or frozen to death.

shouted one of the gunners, "see me take a chimney!" He put a slow match to the powder vent and his shot knocked a boat's stack into the river. At this point, the booming of cannon was continuous and deafening, and commands had to be given by signs.

All four Federal boats, still driving stubbornly forward against the current, were in trouble now. A newspaperman aboard the *Louisville* reported multiple hits and wrote: "A shell raked us from bow to stern, passed through the wheel house, emerged, dropped and exploded in the river just at our stern. Then a ten-inch solid shot entered our starboard bow-port, demolished a gun-carriage, killed three men and wounded four others, traversed the entire length of the boat and sank into the river in our wake. Then a shell came shrieking through the air, striking fair into our forward starboard port, killing one man, wounding two, and then passed aft, sundering our rudder chains, and rendering the boat unmanageable. We were compelled to drop astern."

Aboard the *St. Louis*, Foote was wounded in the foot by a shell that crashed into the pilothouse, killed the pilot and carried away the wheel. Out of control, the ship drifted downstream after the *Louisville*. The *Pittsburgh* and the *Carondelet* took a pounding; hulls breached, they shipped water. The *Pittsburgh* was in danger of sinking bow first until her captain shifted her guns to the rear. Then, in turning, the vessel collided with the *Carondelet*, shearing her starboard rudder. Walke tried frantically to rig emergency steering as he drifted downstream stern to. But he had the presence of mind to keep his bow guns blazing away in the hope that the smoke would provide a screen from the fort's guns.

All this while, not a single man in the waterside batteries had been hurt. The Confederates watched the boats drift helplessly downstream and, said one, "a shout of exultation leaped from the lips of every soldier in the fort."

That night Grant, who had watched the debacle from the riverbank below the fort, sent General Halleck a not very confident message saying that he might have to besiege Donelson after all. The battle had been seriously miscalculated. Foote had come a cropper because he had pushed to nearly point-blank range, where, having to fire at maximum elevation to reach the batteries high above them, his guns with their arcing trajectories tended to overshoot their targets. Since his heavier guns had longer range than the Confederates', he probably could have shattered the waterside batteries while staying beyond the reach of most enemy cannon. However, he had triumphed at Fort Henry by the same tactic of driving in close.

The resounding Confederate victory over the gunboats did little to lighten the profound gloom that had settled on Donelson's three brigadiers. They already had decided that the fort was a trap and would cost them their army if they did not get out. Their pessimism had been bolstered by a somber prebattle message from Johnston: "If you lose the fort, bring your troops to Nashville if possible." They were relieved to note that Johnston had completed his retreat to Nashville, since this freed them of their rearguard assignment. And since they had been planning a breakout when the gunboats attacked, they went right on planning it despite their unexpected victory.

The generals' plan was to shatter Grant's

Aboard the Federal ironclad *Carondelet*, the port rifled gun blows up during a futile gunboat attack on Fort Donelson on February 14, 1862. "When it exploded, it knocked us all down," wrote a member of the gun crew, "wounding over a dozen men and spreading dismay and confusion among us."

investment with a sudden hammer blow and break out to the south toward a road that led to Nashville. Gideon Pillow's men, on the Confederate left facing General McClernand's division, would attack at dawn. Simon Buckner would leave a single regiment, the 13th Tennessee Infantry, in the trenches to the right, facing General Smith's division, and move the bulk of his men to the center. Once Pillow had rolled the Federal troops back, Buckner would strike the hinge and hold the door open while Pillow's division marched out to safety. Then Buckner would follow, fighting a rear-guard action to make sure that the bulk of the army escaped intact

to fight again on more opportune ground.

Another winter storm spread misery that night, and a howling wind covered the noise the Confederates made as they moved into position to attack. They were ready when dawn broke in a clear sky, showing ground covered with fresh snow and tree limbs sheathed in ice.

Grant got up before dawn at his farmhouse headquarters to visit Foote at his anchorage below Donelson. He issued orders for his division commanders to hold their positions and do nothing to bring on an engagement—an obvious warning against a repetition of McClernand's unauthorized attack. Grant was thinking of besieging Donelson; he was not concerned about a Confederate breakout. As he later admitted, "I had no idea that there would be any engagement on land unless I brought it on myself." Without designating a second-in-command, he set out over roads that had been muddy and now were frozen hard and slick. He and a single orderly clattered past the men of the 20th Ohio, who were on the march toward Donelson. Minutes later the Ohioans heard firing begin in the distance.

Pillow's Confederates had attacked, their main blow landing on McClernand's extreme right, near the river, where the troops were thinnest. Though the Federals had no warning, they were not caught entirely by surprise; the men were too cold to sleep, so they were up kindling fires at first light, roasting breakfast bacon that supply wagons had brought up overnight. Said Lieutenant Harland of the 18th Illinois: "The Rebels opened fire on our pickets and run them in. We formed the line of battle expecting only a slight skirmish, but when we came to the brow of the hill we seen our mistake for we could see them coming in columns of regiments and the firing was terrific, beyond description. We lay flat on the ground waiting orders to commence firing. At last we got them and we poured a fire into them that I think thinned their ranks considerable."

That crashing volley stopped Pillow's men and threw them back, but the break was only momentary. They picked themselves up and charged again and rocked the Federals back. The woods were dense and the ground very rough. Formal lines dissolved into strings of skirmishes. Units on both sides quickly lost touch with one another and men waged countless little individual fights, bit-

General John B. Floyd, the Confederate commander at Fort Donelson, was accused of having misappropriated $870,000 as President Buchanan's Secretary of War—an accusation portrayed as fact in the Northern cartoon above. Actually, Floyd had demanded a trial, at which point the charges were dropped for lack of evidence.

terly contesting each rock and sheltering tree. Streaks of flame darted from trees, and men ran from rock to rock, threw themselves down on the run, fired and rolled onto their backs to reload.

It was nine o'clock before Pillow regained enough control to form an organized line, and soon afterward McClernand's troops were retreating, driven off by dismounted cavalrymen, who had worked their way around McClernand's open right flank. The horsemen were commanded by that toughminded Tennessee planter and slave trader, Nathan Bedford Forrest.

McClernand, having lost his hard fight, sent a desperate message to Lew Wallace, whose division was next to his in Grant's extended battle line. The mounted messenger, a major, reined up before Wallace and said: "The general told me to tell you the whole

rebel force in the fort massed against him in the night. Our ammunition is giving out. We are losing ground. No one can tell what will be the result if we don't get immediate help.''

But orders were orders. Wallace sent a lieutenant to the farmhouse headquarters to ask for permission to move. Soon the man returned: Grant was still away and no one at headquarters had—or was willing to take—the authority to change his orders.

"Our men began to fall dead and wounded," Lieutenant Harland said. "Our ammunition gave out after firing three hours." Men tore the cartridge boxes from the bodies of men who had fallen; Confederate and Federal bodies were scattered in the wood, staining the snow red. The Federals were giving way, but not in rout; they moved back foot by foot, loading and firing as they went.

Another messenger galloped up to Wal-lace. "Our right flank is turned," he cried. Wallace saw that the man was in tears. Ammunition was low and the right was being pressed back on the center. "The whole army is in danger."

Wallace now had to act on his own authority, and he quickly released one of his two brigades to McClernand. Just then Grant's assistant adjutant general, Captain John A. Rawlins, rode up to Wallace. As they talked, stragglers were running from the direction of the front. Wallace then heard more horses' hoofs, and he wrote that an officer, "bare-headed and wild-eyed, rode madly up the road crying, 'We're cut to pieces!' "

Rawlins was enraged by this hysterical exhibition. "Jerking a revolver from his holster," Wallace said, "he would have shot the frantic wretch had I not caught his hand." As if to confirm the panicky officer, an orderly dashed up and told Wallace that McClernand's troops were in full retreat—"a stampede!"

The brigade from Wallace's division, under Colonel Charles Cruft, was moving up against this stream. Cruft's men were wildly excited, and soon a Kentucky regiment in his brigade saw figures ahead and opened fire. In fact, they were firing into the backs of the beleaguered men of the 18th Illinois. Lieutenant Harland was on the receiving end of that fire. "The 25th Kaintucky," he wrote, "then busily retreated, leaving us to draw off as best we could under a heavy cross fire from their infantry and a severe fire from their batteries of shells, grape and canister which killed a great many."

A Federal disaster was in the making by the time Grant finished his talk with Foote. The general was rowed ashore from Foote's flagship and found an aide awaiting him

General Ulysses S. Grant, on horseback *(center)*, watches his troops advance on Fort Donelson, atop the distant ridge. Two black servants carry a wounded Federal

officer (*right*) to an impromptu field hospital behind an artillery battery (*left*). The white-bearded horseman is Colonel Joseph D. Webster, Grant's chief of staff.

"white with fear." Grant listened to the bad news and then set out at a gallop over seven miles of icy road. It was about 1 p.m. when he reached Wallace's position, and he did not like what he found there. "I saw the men standing in knots talking in the most excited manner. No officer seemed to be giving any directions. The soldiers had their muskets but no ammunition, while there were tons of it close at hand."

Grant rode up to Generals Wallace and McClernand, his face flushed with anger, his hand crumpling pieces of paper convulsively. Grant heard McClernand complain, "This army wants a head," to which he replied, "It seems so." Then he said calmly, "Gentlemen, the position on the right must be retaken."

He heard soldiers saying that the enemy troops had come out with three days' rations in their haversacks; the soldiers assumed that the Confederates would fight until their rations gave out. But Grant read the facts differently. He reasoned that men did not carry rations when they charged unless they intended to keep on going, and therefore that this was a breakout attempt. Furthermore, he concluded that the Confederates were able to hit so hard on his right because they had pulled troops from his left, where General Smith's division stood untouched. And the Confederate push seemed to be slowing. No doubt this indicated that their breakout way was open, but more important it meant that they were exhausted.

Grant had understood intuitively that this was one of those fleeting, decisive moments that sometimes occur in battle. Both sides were reeling and, he told an aide, "The one who attacks first now will be victorious." And he added, "The enemy will have

to be in a hurry if he gets ahead of me."

Grant told Wallace and McClernand to advance and retake the lost ground. And he spread the word himself, galloping down the line with his aide, shouting, "Fill your cartridge boxes, quick, and get into line; the enemy is trying to escape and he must not be permitted to do so." This, Grant said later, "acted like a charm. The men only wanted someone to give them a command."

Grant sent a hasty message to Foote asking for a gunboat demonstration against the fort and rode off to Smith's position. "General Smith," Grant said without preamble, "all has failed on our right. You must take Fort Donelson."

Smith unfolded his long legs and stood up. "I will do it," he said, and Grant noted gratefully that "the general was off in an incredibly short time."

As Grant realized, what had started as a Confederate breakout was now very close to a Confederate triumph. The Federal line was pushed back at right angles to its original position and the Confederates, though tired and battered, had the momentum for victory. On that momentum they might smash Grant's army, or they could still carry out the original plan and escape.

They did neither. General Pillow, having opened the escape hatch, unaccountably ordered the troops back to the fort to regroup. The more professional Buckner, whose men, as planned, had just secured a road that led to Nashville, protested that they must move out in spite of their exhaustion and disarray. Pillow ordered Buckner to pull back. Buckner refused. General Floyd appeared. He listened to Buckner and agreed: They would escape. Pillow took him aside. He listened and again agreed:

They would return to their entrenchments.

In the midst of this, General Smith's advance began against the Confederate right, where Buckner had left the 30th Tennessee Infantry to guard the earthworks. As the firing began, Buckner rushed his men back to meet the assault.

The unbloodied 2nd Iowa was at the head of Smith's attacking column. The men were eager for their first battle and grew nervous with anticipation as they listened to the rattle of musketry and boom of artillery off to the right. Then General Smith rode up and gave orders from the saddle. "He told us to rely upon the bayonet," wrote a young soldier named John G. Greenawalt, "and not to fire a shot until the enemy's works were reached and his lines broken. Little was said. We stood silently in thought, awaiting the order to advance." Greenawalt looked around and saw his handsome company commander, Captain Jack Slaymaker, standing with bowed head as if in prayer.

Then they started. They moved through a narrow strip of woods that hid them from the enemy's works. Then, Greenawalt said, "the command, 'By the right flank!' brought us squarely fronting and in open view of the Confederate earthworks on the brow of the hill, and now 200 yards away the enemy's first volleys of fire pass over our heads. We press forward. They get the range and the shots begin to tell." Felled timber slowed the Iowans but they pressed on toward the Confederates.

General Smith, with his sword in hand and his long mustache flying in the wind, ranged far ahead, looking back now and then to make sure that he was being followed. "I was nearly scared to death," a soldier later said, "but I saw the old man's white mustache over his shoulder and went on."

"Damn you, gentlemen, I see skulkers, I'll have none here," the general roared. "Come on, you volunteers, come on. This is your chance. You volunteered to be killed for love of country and now you can be!" Greenawalt saw the men of the 2nd Iowa color guard picked off one by one: "Sergeant Doolittle fell early in the charge pierced by four balls. Corporal Page took the flag but soon fell dead. Corporal Churcher took it next and fell with a wound which cost his arm. Corporal Weaver next fell mortally wounded, and Corporal Robinson was next to fall, shot in the face. Corporal Twombly seized the flag, was knocked down by a spent ball, but, recovering, carried the flag to the end of the fight, the only man on his feet at the close."

Greenawalt saw Captain Slaymaker fall dead. Then "I sank down and for the first time realized that the balls were flying pretty thick. I heard one or two strike the log I fell on, and only remember crawling down on the lower side of it, when all consciousness passed from me. When I recovered, I found myself a half-mile in the rear, the surgeon cutting a ball out of my right hip."

By then the bayonet-wielding Federals had gone up and over the earthworks, and the single regiment that Buckner had left in place was forced out and back. For two hours that afternoon, Buckner's troops tried with repeated charges to retake the position they had lost, but Smith's men could not be budged. Union artillery was placed to command the rest of the Confederate entrenchments. And on the right, Federal soldiers were moving forward to reclaim most of the ground lost in the morning. They found the Confederates withdrawing from posi-

The 2nd Iowa Regiment, under Brigadier General Charles Smith's command, storms Fort Donelson's entrenchments on the afternoon of February 15, 1862. General Grant ordered this charge to relieve the pressure of the Confederate assault at the other end of the battle line.

tions taken at great cost only hours before.

At the Dover Inn, the three Confederate brigadiers gathered to compare notes. Floyd and Pillow were still elated over their early success; they wired General Johnston at Nashville that they had won a great victory. Buckner, on the other hand, considered the army's position desperate. Angrily he told Pillow and Floyd they should have marched out as planned while the way was open. Floyd retorted that the plan always had been to wait for nightfall and then march out unobserved, and he was ready to start now.

But now reports came in that Federal campfires were burning again in their old positions, just out of sharpshooter range. The breakout had been for naught, the generals realized, and they agreed with Buckner that their men lacked the strength for another battle.

Around one o'clock the generals summoned Nathan Bedford Forrest, who was amazed to find that they were discussing the surrender of the army. The cavalryman protested. The Federals had not occupied their extreme right by the river, he said, and he believed the way out was still open. He sent two scouts to examine the ground. They soon returned shaking with cold and reported seeing no Federal troops, though the fires were burning. Forrest insisted that the wind—or wounded men on both sides —had stirred the fires. But the generals' minds were made up.

Forrest protested again. Let them fight their way out—he would guarantee to cover their rear and hold off any Federal cavalry attacks. His men had found a little-used river road that definitely was open. In one place the road was under three feet of cold floodwater for about 100 yards. But the

generals refused. Floyd had talked to his medical director, who said that troops could not survive such a wade. (Neither side understood this early in the War how much men could endure.)

What to do, then? "It would be wrong," Buckner said, "to subject the army to a virtual massacre when no good would come from the sacrifice." He voted to surrender. Floyd and Pillow agreed as to the men but not as to themselves. Pillow believed that his capture would be a Confederate disaster. And Floyd feared the Federals would try him on old charges that as United States Secretary of War he had made fraudulent deals and had treasonously shifted Federal arms to Southern arsenals, where they could be seized by secessionists.

An officer on Pillow's staff, Major Gus A. Henry Jr., recorded what happened next: "General Floyd then spoke out, and said that he would not surrender the command or himself.

"General Buckner remarked that, if placed in command, he would surrender the command and share its fate.

"General Floyd then said, 'General Buckner, if I place you in command, will you allow me to get out as much of my brigade as I can?'

"General Buckner replied, 'I will, provided you do so before the enemy receives my proposition for capitulation.'

"General Floyd then turned to General Pillow and said, 'I turn the command over, sir.'

"General Pillow replied promptly, 'I pass it.'

"General Buckner said, 'I assume it. Give me pen, ink and paper, and send for a bugler.'"

Lieutenant Colonel Nathan Bedford Forrest leads a long line of Confederate troopers across an icy backwater of the Cumberland River during their escape from Fort Donelson before dawn on February 16, 1862. Despite the snow, a cold, biting wind and sheer exhaustion, the men covered the 75 miles to Nashville in just two days.

Whereupon Forrest growled in disgust, "I did not come here for the purpose of surrendering my command," and stomped out. A few minutes later he had his officers assemble. He was going out, he told them, or would die trying; everyone who wanted to accompany him was welcome. His entire regiment went, starting down the river road with many a horseman carrying a foot soldier behind him.

Buckner's men, who felt they had won every time they met the Federals, were outraged to see a messenger departing under a white flag, obviously with a surrender offer of some sort. They tried to stop the man but he persisted. An hour later General Smith was at the farmhouse headquarters with Buckner's message.

Grant got out of the feather bed and drew on his trousers. Smith warmed his backside by the fire. He asked if anyone had a drink. Grant's friend and physician, John H. Brinton, produced his flask and Smith took a long pull.

Grant read Buckner's proposal to discuss surrender terms. He had personal reasons for agreeing to talk; Buckner was an old friend who had loaned him money in New York when he had returned broke from California after resigning his commission in 1854. "Well," Grant said to Smith, "what do you think?"

"No terms with traitors, by God!"

Grant sat down and dashed off a message that would make him famous. Then he read it out loud.

Sir:

Yours of this date, proposing armistice and appointment of commissioners to settle terms of capitulation, is just received. No terms except unconditional and immediate surrender can be accepted. I propose to move immediately upon your works.

I am, sir, very respectfully, your obedient servant,

U. S. Grant

Smith barked, "By God, it couldn't be better!"

A bit later, Buckner opened Grant's answer. By then, Pillow and Floyd had slipped away by boat. Forrest was gone with his cavalry; he lost not a man crossing that water. Hundreds and perhaps thousands of infantrymen escaped as well. Even if Grant's brusque message had provoked Buckner to fight again, it was too late. Buckner replied stiffly that he had no choice but to accept Grant's "ungenerous and unchivalrous terms."

In the hospital camp that Sunday morning, John Greenawalt and other wounded men of the 2nd Iowa "heard great and continuous cheering." It began in Smith's division as word of Buckner's surrender spread through the army. Soon the 2nd Iowa's flag, which Corporal Twombly had brought through the battle, was raised over Fort Donelson to a 13-gun salute. Even the weather smiled on victory; it turned warm and loosed rivulets of melted snow.

When Grant reached the Dover Inn, he found Lew Wallace there ahead of him, eating a breakfast of corn bread and coffee with Buckner and his staff. Buckner had been wondering whether a captured West Pointer would be treated as a traitor or simply as a prisoner of war. Grant set his mind at rest. They fell to chatting, and soon the question arose of General Pillow's grasp of the martial arts.

"Where is he now?" Grant asked.

"Gone," Buckner said. "He thought you'd rather get hold of him than any other man in the Southern Confederacy."

"Oh," said Grant, "if I had got him, I'd let him go again. He will do us more good commanding you fellows."

Later Grant took Buckner aside and, repaying that favor done him long ago, offered the use of his purse as the defeated Confederate went into captivity.

The Federal victory at Fort Donelson touched off celebrations all across the North. At the Union Merchants Exchange in St. Louis, speculators stopped work to sing patriotic songs and then went to Halleck's headquarters to cheer. In Cincinnati, said a newspaper, "Everybody was shaking hands with everybody else, and bewhiskered men embraced each other as if they were lovers."

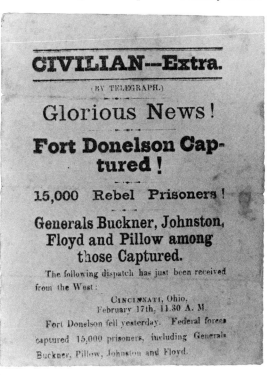

CIVILIAN--Extra.

(BY TELEGRAPH.)

Glorious News!

Fort Donelson Captured!

15,000 Rebel Prisoners!

Generals Buckner, Johnston, Floyd and Pillow among those Captured.

The following dispatch has just been received from the West:

CINCINNATI, Ohio, February 17th, 11.30 A. M.

Fort Donelson fell yesterday. Federal forces captured 15,000 prisoners, including Generals Buckner, Pillow, Johnston and Floyd.

This hastily printed Northern broadside exaggerates the extent of the Federal victory at Fort Donelson. Of the four generals said to have been captured, only Buckner was actually taken prisoner.

The *Chicago Tribune* noted that "Chicago reeled mad with joy."

Grant became an overnight hero to a nation badly in need of heroes. The core of his message to Buckner, coinciding with his initials, earned him the name "Unconditional Surrender" Grant. Newspapers reported that he had gone to victory with a cigar clamped in his teeth, and so many admirers sent him cigars that he gave up his pipe.

General Halleck offered Grant no congratulations. Instead he telegraphed Washington: MAKE BUELL, GRANT AND POPE MAJOR-GENERALS AND GIVE ME COMMAND IN THE WEST. I ASK THIS IN RETURN FOR FORTS HENRY AND DONELSON. Lincoln answered by promoting Grant to major general and ignoring Halleck's other recommendations. That made Grant second only to Halleck in the West, which had hardly been Halleck's intention. But Lincoln's historical judgment was sound. Fort Donelson was the largest battle yet fought in the West and it would prove to be among the most significant of the War.

There was a nasty little epilogue to Grant's promotion. Halleck, angered by a lapse in communications, ordered Grant to remain at Fort Henry and to place C. F. Smith in command of the expedition up the Tennessee. Fortunately the damage was soon undone. Lincoln mollified Halleck by giving him the overall command in the West, and to rescue a fighting general, the President in effect told Halleck to press charges against Grant or to drop the matter. A month after his victory at Donelson, Grant was back in the field.

On the Confederate side, many believed that their war was lost at Donelson; indeed the fall of the fort opened the way south and led

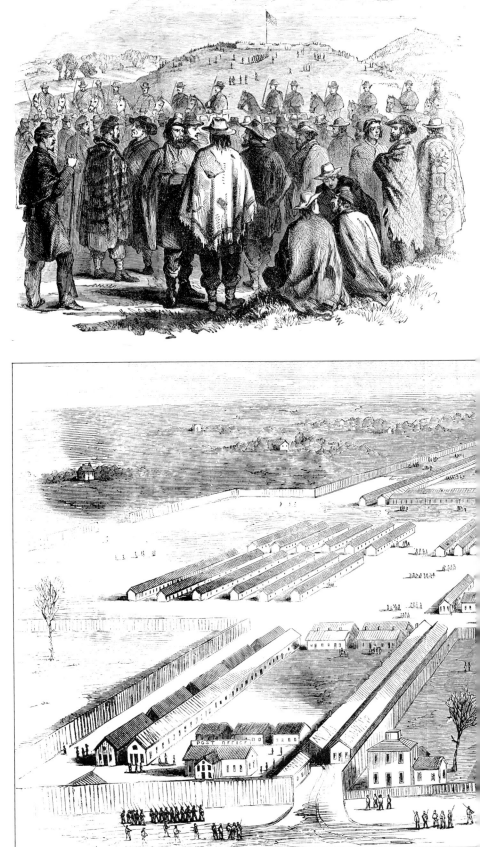

Shivering Confederate prisoners mill about at Fort Donelson on February 17, 1862, the day after they surrendered to Grant's army. Most of the captives were interned at Camp Douglas (below), **near Chicago.**

Sprawling Camp Douglas, originally used as a Federal training base for Western regiments, was converted into a prison to accommodate the huge bag of Confederate soldiers captured at Forts Donelson and Henry. Each wooden barracks measured 90 by 24 feet, contained a kitchen and housed about 170 men.

to the fatal splitting of the Confederacy, which had been the Union plan all along. The Confederates also suffered a devastating immediate loss. According to Federal estimates, Grant's men had taken 12,000 to 15,000 prisoners, 20,000 stand of arms, 48 pieces of artillery, 17 heavy guns, from 2,000 to 4,000 horses and large quantities of commissary stores. The Confederates had lost more than 450 men killed and 1,500 wounded—somewhat lighter losses than the Federals' 500 men killed and 2,100 wounded.

Johnston himself summed up the terrible price in a short message to Beauregard:

"At 2 a.m. today Fort Donelson surrendered. We lost all." Later that morning, while Sunday church bells were ringing in celebration of Floyd's early victory message, Johnston told Governor Harris to get the state records out of Nashville. The Yankees were coming and the Confederate army must abandon the city.

The Federals heading for town were not Grant's, however; they belonged to the command of General Don Carlos Buell. Under pressure from Washington, Buell had proceeded south from Louisville with the bulk of his 45,000-man army and occupied Bowl-

ing Green after the Confederates abandoned it. Buell intended to take Nashville and to stand ready there to cooperate with Grant in some future operation. He was in no great hurry, and reports of his progress had preceded him to Nashville.

In the city, it was said that 35,000 ravening Yankees were approaching, and that gunboats would shortly arrive to shell Nashville into rubble. People milled about the streets, circulating rumors, loading what they could carry into wagons and fleeing south. Departing trains were jammed with men, some even riding on the roofs. Entrepreneurs hired out their wagons and teams for up to $25 an hour.

First Lieutenant Basil Duke, one of Johnston's officers, wrote: "Some wept at the thought of abandoning the city to a fate which they esteemed as dreadful as utter destruction; and many, infuriated, loudly advocated burning it to the ground, that the enemy might have nothing of it but its ashes. Crowds of soldiers were mingled with the citizens, who thronged the streets all night; and yells, curses, shots rang on all sides."

The people needed someone to blame, and within a day their reverent admiration for Johnston had turned into contempt and something like hatred. This sense of outrage leaped across the South. A Kentucky congressman wired President Davis that Johnston's errors were greater than those of ANY OTHER GENERAL WHO EVER PRECEDED HIM IN ANY COUNTRY, and a group of Tennesseans went to Richmond to demand Johnston's removal "because he is no general." Davis dismissed them with a curt comment: "Gentlemen, I know Sidney Johnston well. If *he* is not a general, we had better give up the war for we have no general."

Johnston bore this abuse with dignity. To Davis, he wrote, "I observed silence, as it seemed to me to be the best way to serve the cause. The test of merit in my profession, with the people, is success. It is a hard rule, but I think it right."

The retreating army lumbered through Nashville, its wagons and guns turning rain-swept streets to seas of mud. The soldiers were heading southeast, to rendezvous at Murfreesboro and then continue on to make a stand in Alabama, south of the Tennessee River. Johnston went with them, leaving Floyd in charge—and Nashville in chaos.

The mayor had promised the citizens any leftover army stores, and now mobs of desperate people began taking what they wanted by force. Lieutenant Duke reported, "Excitement and avarice seemed to stimulate the people to preternatural strength. I saw an old woman, whose appearance indicated the extremest decrepitude, staggering under a load of meat which I would have hardly thought a quartermaster's mule could carry."

Then Nathan Bedford Forrest rode into Nashville at the head of his column. He took over from Floyd the job of restoring law and order. He appealed to the populace to think of their patriotic duty, and when that did not work he lined up his men and galloped into the mob, swinging the flat of his big saber in his left hand and scattering people before him. He used a fire hose to keep the mob away from the warehouse in Public Square while his men emptied it.

Forrest commandeered every wagon he could find, and before he was finished he got out large quantities of weapons and ammunition, as well as 250,000 pounds of bacon, at least 600 boxes of army clothing, and hundreds of wagonloads of flour and commissary stores. He dismantled some of the Nashville foundry's precious machinery for rifling cannon and shipped it with other ordnance equipment to Atlanta. Then, at the last moment, he and his men went drifting down the road to Murfreesboro as the first Federal troops entered Nashville. A few Federals followed him, and Forrest turned and bloodied them; they need not think that tracking Sidney Johnston's army was going to be easy.

Nearly a third of Johnston's men were sick, suffering from the effects of those winter storms that had brought such misery to Donelson. But he kept his troops moving south; and by the time they crossed the Tennessee River in northern Alabama and were once again in country that could be defended, Johnston had restored their hope and their *élan*. The War was not over nor the fighting done.

Beauregard, meanwhile, had headed west to take charge of the withdrawal there and

How a Soldier Saved His Colors

When Fort Donelson fell to Federal forces on February 16, 1862, Andrew S. Payne, color-bearer of the 14th Mississippi Infantry Regiment, vowed that he would never give up his unit's battle flag to the Yankees. It was a beautiful hand-painted flag, presented by a group of patriotic ladies to the Shubuta Rifles, one of the regiment's companies. More important, the regiment had fought hard and well under the flag before being forced to surrender: Seventeen men were killed and 85 were wounded in a futile effort to retake a portion of the entrenchments of the fort. Payne refused to dishonor his comrades by giving up the flag.

Before the prisoners were shipped off to Camp Douglas, near Chicago (*pages 96-97*), Payne cut out the center of the flag and sewed it into the lining of his coat; thus he carefully preserved the emblems on both sides of the flag: Lady Liberty (*right*) dressed in a toga, holding a picture of Jefferson Davis in one hand and a beribboned sword in the other; and on the reverse, an eagle with its claws about a snake that had invaded its nest of eaglets in a magnolia tree. The flag was still concealed in Payne's coat when, on October 16, 1862, he and most of his comrades were sent back to Mississippi in an exchange of prisoners. There, at last, Payne returned the flag to his regiment.

The 51st Regiment of Ohio Volunteers holds a dress parade in Nashville, Tennessee, on March 4, 1862. The first captured capital of a Confederate state, Nashville was to remain an advanced base and headquarters for the Federal operations in the West.

fell sick on the way. Stopping at Jackson, Tennessee, he set up headquarters, called General Polk to his bedside and told him that his fortifications at Columbus must be abandoned. Reluctantly Polk began withdrawing his men.

As Beauregard's health began to improve, he conceived an offensive. Without consulting Johnston, he appealed to the governors of Southern states for men and arms, and vowed that with a new army he would sweep north, seize the mouths of the Cumberland and the Tennessee, attack Cairo and threaten St. Louis. "What say you to this brilliant program?" he wrote to Major General Earl Van Dorn in Arkansas by way of soliciting his assistance. "We must do something soon or die in the attempt."

Van Dorn cared little for Beauregard's plan but suggested one of his own that would also threaten St. Louis. A famous Indian fighter and an elegant West Pointer in his early forties, he had united the contentious Confederate factions in Arkansas and proposed to lead about 16,000 men north to invade Missouri. A small Federal army stood in his way, but if he could bowl it over and attack St. Louis, the whole equation of the War would change; Grant would be forced to pull back and Johnston would have time to regain command of the situation.

But as it turned out, this small solution to the problem was doomed. General Halleck and his headquarters staff in St. Louis scraped up supplies and ammunition for that small Federal army—11,000 men under Brigadier General Samuel R. Curtis. Then, in early March, Curtis met Van Dorn in the shadow of a steep little mountain known as Pea Ridge. Van Dorn was soundly defeated and thrown back to the Arkansas River.

Johnston and Beauregard proceeded with plans to strike a massive blow at Grant's army. Events now were making that attack seem more and more possible. The South, shocked by Donelson and Nashville, was at last responding with troops and weapons. It was time to concentrate and get ready.

As his main concentration point, Johnston chose Corinth, Mississippi, a strategic rail junction 20 miles inland from the big bend of the Tennessee. Johnston could not afford to retreat any farther: If the rail lines crossing at Corinth fell to the Union, Memphis would be cut off from the East and Mobile would lose its communication link into the Tennessee Valley. Johnston knew that Corinth was bound to be the next Union objective. What better place for him to mass his troops and launch a devastating surprise attack?

Confederate troops streamed into Corinth from every direction. Nearly all of Johnston's men converged there; the prime exception was 5,000 of Polk's force, who were sent to help defend Island No. 10, a fortified speck of real estate blocking the Mississippi near New Madrid. Ten thousand men came from Pensacola under Major General Braxton Bragg and 5,000 more from New Orleans under Brigadier General Daniel Ruggles. Johnston later called in Van Dorn and his army, but it was too late. Adequate transportation could not be arranged in time to make them available when they were desperately needed in the great battle that lay ahead.

Nevertheless, nearly 40,000 soldiers were gathered in Corinth in early April of 1862. Things were coming together at last, Johnston felt. Now was the time for the Confederates to make their move in the West.

101

After the capture of nearby Fort Donelson, a small Federal garrison stands guard in an encampment on the banks of the Cumberland River. Several such forces

were left behind at strategic points to hold northwestern Tennessee as Federal armies carried the War south.

"The Devil's Own Day"

4

Boatload by boatload in the third week of March, General Grant's army moved up the Tennessee River and debarked at a tiny port called Pittsburg Landing to prepare for an attack on Corinth, 22 miles inland. Grant, as ever aggressive, was anxious to maintain the momentum of his victory at Fort Donelson and strike the Confederates while they were still reeling. But Halleck, as ever cautious, checked the advance until reinforcements could reach Grant. Don Carlos Buell's 55,000-man Army of the Ohio had occupied Nashville, and on March 16, Halleck directed Buell to march his troops the 122 miles to Savannah, Tennessee, a small town nine miles downstream from Pittsburg Landing. Halleck told Grant to risk no engagement until Buell joined him.

Buell was slowed down by the retreating Confederates, who burned bridges in their wake. Grant chafed at the delay. He sent telegrams to Halleck urging an immediate attack before the enemy regrouped. Halleck did not respond. So Grant fretted and fumed to get on with the attack—and completely discounted the possibility that Sidney Johnston's forces might attack him first.

During the delay, Grant spent much of his time planning the campaign at his headquarters, a mansion in Savannah. He had given command of the encampment to an old associate who had just rejoined his army, Brigadier General William Tecumseh Sherman.

Sherman was 42, a tall, thin man with sunken temples and sandy red hair and beard. He was eccentric, brilliant, often uncertain and intensely nervous. A West Pointer, he was stationed in California during the Mexican War; there he and Henry Halleck became friends. Thereafter, Sherman became a banker in California, ran a military academy in Louisiana (it grew into Louisiana State University) and was seeking the presidency of a trolley line in St. Louis when the War began. He served creditably as a brigade commander in the Federal disaster at Bull Run and then preceded Buell as commanding officer at Louisville. After he was relieved for what amounted to a nervous breakdown, Halleck came to his rescue, sending him home to rest and then giving him easy assignments. Three months later Sherman had recovered and returned to the field as a division commander.

Grant was glad to have Sherman as his right-hand man. Though Sherman had been senior to Grant while they both were brigadiers, he had cooperated readily in a subordinate position during Grant's campaign against the river forts. This willing suspension of the privilege of rank was extraordinary and Grant appreciated it. The two men thus formed a lifelong friendship and a potent military partnership.

Both Sherman and Grant regarded the Pittsburg Landing site as a good defensive position. The army had bivouacked on a rough plateau that rolled westward from high bluffs overlooking the Tennessee River. The encampment was protected not only by the Tennessee but by its tributaries, Owl and Snake Creeks in the north and Lick Creek to the south, all of them in flood stage and 25 feet deep in places. The terrain was heavily forested, dotted with farmland and orchards, and slashed by steep ravines.

This bugle was shot from the hands of Frederick Barnhart, a private in Company B of the 15th Indiana, as he was sounding the call to battle at Shiloh. He retrieved and kept the instrument as a memento of one of the bloodiest clashes of the War.

Though the area was easy to defend, the Federals made little effort to organize a defense. Grant, like most West Pointers of the period, believed that the protection of trenches engendered cowardice. Sherman, like Grant, did not anticipate a Confederate attack and took only the most basic precautions: His line of outposts was shallow, extending only a few hundred yards from his camps; no trenches or earthworks were dug. And since Sherman usually assigned camping areas to units as they arrived, it happened by chance that the men who would take the first shock of the Confederate attack had seen no fighting, while the veterans were well to the rear or off the field entirely.

Sherman's green division held the advance position about four miles inland from the landing, more or less on the right, though he had posted one brigade, under Colonel David Stuart, on the far left, near Lick Creek. Sherman set up headquarters near a crossroads and a one-room log church erected by Methodists a decade earlier and now seldom used. This cracked and weathered hut would give its Biblical name, meaning "place of peace," to the bloody battle to come: Shiloh.

To Sherman's immediate left was another green division, commanded by Brigadier General Benjamin M. Prentiss, an Illinois lawyer and Mexican War veteran. Together, these divisions would form the front line. To the rear of Sherman were Brigadier General McClernand's Donelson veterans. Next to McClernand was a division led by Brigadier General Stephen A. Hurlbut, a South Carolinian who had migrated to Illinois to practice law. Far to the rear, almost at Pittsburg Landing, was Major General Charles F. Smith's well-trained division. But the old warrior who had led the charge at Donelson was out of action now, felled by an injury. His place had been taken by Brigadier General William H. L. Wallace, who had earned his rank at Donelson. A sixth Federal division, Major General Lew Wallace's veterans of Donelson, was encamped at Crump's Landing, three miles below Savannah and six miles from Pittsburg Landing.

None of the generals took adequate precautions. Picket lines were carelessly placed and casually kept. Cavalry patrols, which would have unmasked a Confederate advance immediately, were carried out irregularly. Halleck's warning came down often: "Don't bring on any general engagement."

If Halleck lacked confidence, Grant had too much. He thought his army was invincible, and he unwisely listened to Confederate deserters who reported that "the great mass of the rank and file are heartily tired." Corinth, Grant told Halleck, "will fall much more easily than Donelson."

The Federal army was ripe for disaster.

At Corinth, Confederate Generals Johnston and Beauregard were working feverishly to shape the incoming regiments of fresh troops

Displaying makeshift weapons, Federal volunteers of the 21st Missouri typify the poorly equipped and inexperienced soldiers who fought at Shiloh. "I have not really one thorough soldier in my army," complained General W. T. Sherman. "They are all green and raw."

into a working army. Johnston realized that he had little time to spare. At 40,000 men, his strength roughly equaled Grant's. But once Buell linked up with Grant, the Federals would outnumber the Confederates by nearly 2 to 1. Thus Johnston's strategy was clear-cut: He had to strike Grant before Buell reached Pittsburg Landing.

Since Beauregard had begun to shape the Army of the Mississippi and was adept at military organization, Johnston let him carve the army into four corps, each with two or more divisions. The officers appointed as corps commanders were distinguished men, though not necessarily in the military field. Major General John C. Breckinridge, who headed a corps of 6,400, had been Vice President of the United States under Buchanan, but he had never led troops in battle. Major

General Leonidas Polk was outstanding as an Episcopal bishop but lacked the experience to make full use of his West Point training; he would command a 9,100-man corps. Major General William J. Hardee, whose corps had 6,800 men, was a capable officer and tactician who had served as commandant of cadets at West Point.

The fourth commander was a puzzling figure. Major General Braxton Bragg, Johnston's adjutant and commander of the Second Corps, with 13,600 men, was a West Pointer who had served with distinction in the Mexican War. Bragg was forceful in the extreme, highly confident—and yet deeply flawed. His foul temper, belligerence and chronic inflexibility had become legend in both armies. Grant liked to tell a joke about the time Bragg did temporary duty as both

Confederates of the Rutledge Rifles, a Tennessee light artillery battery, wear an early-war miscellany of uniforms in a group portrait taken at Nashville. Their commander, Captain A. M. Rutledge, leans on one of the 6-pounder cannon that were later used with telling effect at Shiloh.

company commander and quartermaster. As a company commander, he demanded certain supplies; as quartermaster, he refused. He continued an angry exchange of memorandums in his two roles and finally referred the matter to his post commander. That officer cried, "My God, Mr. Bragg, you have quarreled with every officer in the Army and now you are quarreling with yourself!"

The four corps commanders were still hard at work when, on the evening of April 2, word arrived in Corinth that Buell had cleared the worst obstacles on the march from Nashville and was moving rapidly to join Grant. At 10 p.m. Beauregard scrawled a message, "Now is the moment to advance and strike the enemy at Pittsburg Landing," and sent it to Johnston, who then conferred with Bragg. Perhaps for the sake of argument, Johnston offered objections—the men were insufficiently trained, Major General Earl Van Dorn's army, en route from Arkansas, had not arrived—but Bragg overcame them, insisting that the Confederates must beat Buell to Pittsburg Landing.

Orders to the corps commanders were

drafted immediately: They were to be ready to march at dawn, April 3. One day's march, of about 20 miles, would put them in position to attack at dawn on April 4.

Beauregard sat in bed scribbling down ideas for a plan of attack on scraps of paper and the backs of envelopes. Johnston had suggested a simple order of advance: the Confederate corps moving up side by side in compact columns. The virtue of such a plan was that the inexperienced brigades and regiments could be tightly controlled by each corps commander. Instead, Beauregard concocted a more difficult scheme, suitable only for experienced units: Three corps would attack in three successive lines, each spread clear across a three-mile front. Beauregard's risky plan called for Hardee's men to attack first, then Bragg's huge corps, then Polk's, with Breckinridge in reserve.

Beauregard realized that if the army was to march on April the 3rd and fight on the 4th, there was no time to waste. While his adjutant, Colonel Thomas Jordan, began restating the notes as written orders, he summoned the corps commanders and told them to get started. To manage his heavy traffic on the two roads to Pittsburg Landing, Beauregard planned an intricate pattern of march for his infantry, cavalry, artillery and supply wagons. The roads converged seven miles from the landing at a crossroads, known as Mickey's after a house that stood there. The army was to rendezvous at Mickey's, then move up and form battle lines.

For some reason, Hardee refused to march without the written orders and did not get them until afternoon. Since his corps was to lead, nothing moved until then. Clearly there could be no attack on the 4th. Beauregard pushed back the attack date to the 5th.

Late on the 4th a cold rain began to fall. It came down in torrents all night. The roads turned to mud, guns and wagons sank to their hubs, units became separated, commands intermixed.

Still, Hardee managed to reach Mickey's late on the 4th and formed his battle line on the next day. Bragg's troops drew up behind Hardee, but Bragg could not form the left wing of his battle line because he had lost a division. Johnston sent a message to Bragg asking why his men were not in position. Bragg, who reacted as angrily to questions from above as to infractions from below, answered snappishly that he had sent out a search party.

Noon passed on the 5th, and still Bragg was unready. Johnston looked at his watch and exclaimed: "This is perfectly puerile! This is not war!" He rode to the rear, and

The 9th Mississippi Volunteer
Infantry earned the sobriquet of the
"Fighting Ninth" and a rare accolade
for its part in the Battle of Shiloh
from General Bragg: "Never were
troops and commander more worthy
of each other and their State."

Confederate commanders meet for a war council April 5, 1862, the eve of their attack at Shiloh. They are, from left to right, Generals Beauregard, Polk, Breckinridge, Johnston, Bragg, and Major J. F. Gilmer.

miles behind found Bragg's lost division blocked by some of Polk's troops. Johnston cleared the way and brought the men forward, but by then the sun was setting. The attack was postponed another day, to Sunday, April 6.

Now 40,000 Confederates were poised within two miles of the Federal camps. To preserve any chance of taking the enemy by surprise in the morning, the troops would have to observe strict silence. But the raw young soldiers neglected to obey orders or even use their common sense. When a deer popped from the woods, they whooped. After the rain stopped, they wondered if their powder was dry, and many fired their muskets to find out. Bugles sounded, drums rolled and men yelled. Officers went about trying to hush the men to no avail.

The general clamor, together with word of a clash with a Federal patrol, plunged Beauregard into one of his well-known mer-

curial mood changes. At a roadside conference of the generals, he cried in despair, "Now they will be entrenched to the eyes!" Furthermore, many of the Confederate troops had already exhausted their rations and would be sleeping that night— and fighting tomorrow—on empty bellies. To Johnston's shock, Beauregard argued vehemently for canceling the attack and returning to Corinth.

Johnston rose to the occasion. With majestic calm, he heard Beauregard out and then, General Polk remembered, "remarked that this would never do." Johnston said he doubted that their approach had been detected because there had been no Federal reaction. As for hungry soldiers, they could eat the enemy's supplies. Johnston then closed the conference: "Gentlemen, we shall attack at daylight tomorrow."

As the officers dispersed, Johnston told an aide, "I would fight them if they were a million," adding, "I intend to hammer 'em!"

That night Beauregard heard a drum beating. Angrily he sent an aide to stop the noise. The man was back in a few minutes and reported that the drum was beating in a Federal camp—so close did the two armies lie.

Incredibly, the Federal camp remained somnolent. Its commanders had no idea that an enemy army the size of their own stood just beyond their picket line.

For days, Grant and his generals had had plentiful evidence of the enemy, but had chosen to discount it. On April 4, Confederate cavalry had captured a half-dozen pickets, and a rescue party sent out by Sherman had run head on into the lead element of Hardee's corps. The Federals fled, and later their commander told Sherman that he had seen at least two regiments of Confederate infantry with cavalry and artillery.

"Oh, tut, tut!" Sherman replied. "You militia officers get scared too easily."

All the next day, Saturday, the 5th, the Confederates showed themselves. Confederate cavalrymen were seen watching the 70th Ohio drill. Federal pickets saw brass cannon glinting through the trees, and a group of Federal soldiers were chased from a house only a mile beyond Shiloh Church.

The Confederates threw a scare into the 53rd Ohio, the regiment of Sherman's division camped nearest to the enemy vanguard. One of the greenest outfits in the Army, the 53rd was commanded by an elderly, inept and exceedingly nervous colonel named Jesse J. Appler, who had never learned how to drill his men. On Saturday afternoon Appler's pickets reported suspicious figures in the distance. He sent a detachment to investigate. Shots were heard

and the men rushed back to say that they had been fired on by a "line of men in butternut clothes." This was Hardee's picket line, which had been drawn up to attack since dawn and now was patiently waiting while Sidney Johnston rode back in search of Bragg's missing division.

Horrified, Appler turned out the 53rd and sent his quartermaster to notify Sherman. Minutes later the quartermaster returned and said in a loud voice, "General Sherman says, 'Take your damned regiment back to Ohio. There is no enemy nearer than Corinth!'" Appler's soldiers laughed and broke ranks without waiting for orders; the men resumed their search for wild onions and turkey peas in the warm sunshine.

That day Sherman assured Grant that the Confederates would not attack. Grant wrote Halleck that night, "I have scarcely the faintest idea of an attack being made upon us." Yet Sherman may have had second thoughts; he told a newspaperman that the army was in danger. Startled, the reporter asked why he did not sound the alarm. "Oh," said Sherman, "they'd just say I was crazy again."

Colonel Everett Peabody, a bulky 31-year-old Harvard graduate who commanded a brigade in General Prentiss' division, was warned about the Confederates. He had been told by Major James E. Powell of the 25th Missouri that there was a great sprawl of Confederate campfires beyond the Federal picket lines. So at 3 a.m. on Sunday, April 6, Peabody sent Powell out with a reconnaissance force of about 300 men.

At dawn Powell's troops were a half mile from camp on the edge of a broad farm field. There they ran into Major Aaron B. Hardcastle's 3rd Mississippi Infantry Battalion, the advance guard of Wood's bri-

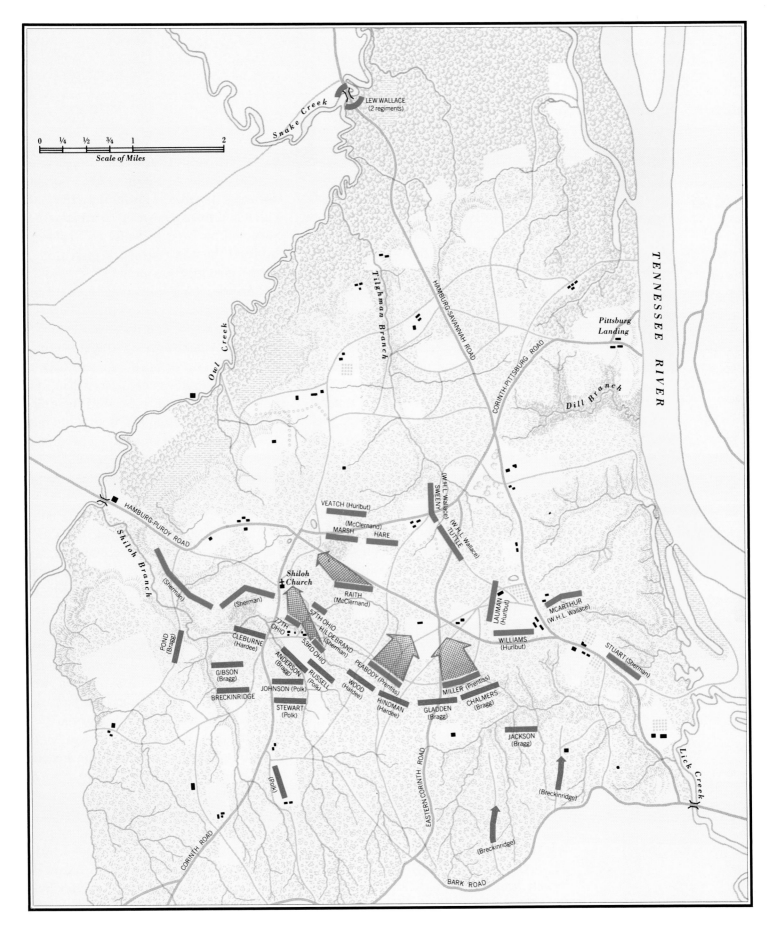

LEW WALLACE
(2 regiments)

Snake Creek

0   ¼   ½   ¾   1   2
Scale of Miles

TENNESSEE RIVER

Tilghman Branch

HAMBURG-SAVANNAH ROAD

Pittsburg
Landing

CORINTH-PITTSBURG ROAD

Owl Creek

Dill Branch

HAMBURG-PURDY ROAD

VEATCH (Hurlbut)

(W.H.L. Wallace)
SWEENY

(McClernand)
MARSH   HARE

TUTTLE
(W.H.L. Wallace)

Shiloh Branch

(Sherman)

Shiloh
Church

RAITH
(McClernand)

LAUMAN
(Hurlbut)

MCARTHUR
(W.H.L. Wallace)

(Sherman)

17TH
OHIO

57TH OHIO
HILDEBRAND
(Sherman)

WILLIAMS
(Hurlbut)

POND
(Bragg)

CLEBURNE
(Hardee)

53RD OHIO

ANDERSON
(Bragg)

RUSSELL
(Polk)

PEABODY (Prentiss)

STUART (Sherman)

GIBSON
(Bragg)

JOHNSON (Polk)

WOOD
(Hardee)

MILLER (Prentiss)

BRECKINRIDGE

STEWART
(Polk)

HINDMAN
(Hardee)

GLADDEN
(Bragg)

CHALMERS
(Bragg)

(Polk)

JACKSON
(Bragg)

Lick Creek

EASTERN CORINTH ROAD

(Breckinridge)

(Breckinridge)

CORINTH ROAD

BARK ROAD

Brigadier General William Tecumseh Sherman, portrayed in this rare photograph about the time of Shiloh, was praised as "a gallant and able officer" in Grant's official battle report to General Halleck. Halleck commended Sherman to Washington and got him promoted to major general of volunteers, retroactive to the first day of the battle.

This map shows the disposition of forces at 9:30 a.m. on April 6, 1862, when three Confederate corps (red) attacked Grant's army all across the Shiloh area, pushing toward the Tennessee River. Surprised in camp, the Federal division under General Prentiss and one of Sherman's brigades, under Colonel Jesse Hildebrand, were put to flight. In the Federal rear, Generals McClernand, Hurlbut and W.H.L. Wallace threw units forward in an effort to stem the Confederate tide.

gade, Hardee's corps. Major Hardcastle's skirmishers fired and fell back. The Federals answered with a volley and moved forward until they saw a long line of Confederate troops kneeling on bushy high ground just ahead. The Mississippians fired and a ball struck down Lieutenant Frederick Klinger of the 25th Missouri. He was the first casualty of Shiloh. For there in the middle of that field, Powell settled down to fight, and the battle was joined. It was the beginning of what General Sherman would soon call "the devil's own day."

Hearing heavy firing, Peabody sent up reinforcements. By the time they reached the front, the whole Confederate line was moving, thousands upon thousands of men advancing at once, and the Federals were falling back, sounding the alarm.

The long drum roll thundered in Peabody's camp, calling the men to grab their weapons and form a line of battle. Just then Prentiss galloped up. He asked angrily if Peabody had provoked this attack. When Peabody admitted that he had sent out a patrol, Prentiss shouted, "Colonel Peabody,

I will hold you personally responsible for bringing on this engagement." Peabody told his general that he was always responsible for his actions. Then he mounted his horse and galloped off to battle.

As the sound of firing reached Sidney Johnston's temporary headquarters on the Pittsburg-Corinth Road, Beauregard was arguing again for abandoning the battle. Johnston cocked an ear to the guns and said, "The battle has opened, gentlemen; it is too late to change our dispositions now."

Johnston told Beauregard to stay in the rear and direct men and supplies as needed, while he rode to the front to lead the men on the battle line. In doing so, Johnston relinquished control of the battle to Beauregard. It was a confusing move. What made it especially confusing was that the two generals had no unified battle plan. Johnston had telegraphed President Davis that the attack would commence with: POLK THE LEFT, BRAGG THE CENTER, HARDEE THE RIGHT, BRECKINRIDGE IN RESERVE. Beyond this, Johnston envisioned a thrust on his right to prevent the Federal army from reaching the Tennessee River and escaping by water. Then the Confederate line would wheel west, pin the enemy against Owl Creek and force a surrender there. Beauregard, for his part, simply wanted to attack in three waves and to push the Federal army straight eastward into the Tennessee. And Johnston apparently never pressed his subordinate to do otherwise.

Johnston rode forward in high spirits. "Tonight we will water our horses in the Tennessee River," he said. Around him long lines of silent men were marching through a heavy white mist that hid the tops of trees. Then the rising sun began burning off the mist and the day was revealed—brilliant, but with a touch of softness in the air, a perfect Tennessee Sunday in spring.

As the battle erupted at dawn, Colonel Appler awakened his adjutant, Lieutenant Ephraim C. Dawes, and the two men stood listening, full of uncertainty. The 53rd's pickets came in, sure that the Confederates were advancing. Then one of Powell's men came by with a bloody arm and bawled, "Get into line—the Rebels are coming!"

Appler deployed his men in a field outside his camp and sent word to Sherman. But the general really did not want to believe the report. This time, when the messenger returned, he whispered Sherman's response: "You must be badly scared over there." Then Dawes saw an awesome sight. Hundreds of men, the sun bright on their gun barrels, were moving directly toward the 53rd's right flank.

Appler cried, "This is no place for us," and led the retreat. His troops raced wildly between their tents. But when they came to a ridge beyond the camp they stopped and sprawled on the brush-covered crest to await the enemy.

Just then Sherman rode up with his orderly, Private Thomas D. Holliday of the 2nd Illinois Cavalry. Sherman thought that the enemy advance was only a reconnaissance in force, but he had to admit it was real. He focused his field glasses. In a moment Confederate skirmishers popped from the brush only 50 yards away. Lieutenant Eustace H. Ball ran toward Sherman, shouting, "General, look to your right!"

Sherman whirled. "My God," he cried, "we are attacked!" He threw up a hand as if to protect himself. The Confederates fired. Holliday, at Sherman's side, was killed in-

Colonel Everett Peabody, whose reconnaissance patrol started the fighting at Shiloh, wrote home prophesying his death in the battle. But the blue-blooded Bostonian assured his parents, "If I go under, it shall be in a manner that the old family shall feel proud of."

stantly, and buckshot hit Sherman's hand.

"Appler," Sherman shouted, "hold your position. I will support you." As Appler watched goggle-eyed, Sherman galloped off.

The Confederates marching on Colonel Appler's camp were intent on capturing the crossroads at Shiloh Church. They were led by Brigadier General Patrick Ronayne Cleburne, who commmanded Hardee's Second Brigade. Cleburne was an Irish immigrant who had served as a British soldier.

On the approach, Cleburne plunged into a sharp ravine, Shiloh Branch, which he had not known about. Immediately the brigade found itself in a swampy morass of mud, tangled vines, saplings and dense underbrush. This barrier split Cleburne's brigade; four of his regiments strayed off, and he was left with only the 6th Mississippi and the 23rd Tennessee, about 1,000 men in all.

Leading this diminished force, Cleburne started up the ravine. Ahead he could see the 53rd Ohio's camp and 50 yards beyond it, on a height, a few rude bulwarks of hay bales and brush hastily made by Appler's men. The Confederates were among the tents when the 53rd opened fire. At the same time, Captain A. C. Waterhouse's battery of the 1st Illinois Light Artillery opened fire with its six rifled guns from a high point on the Federal right. Cleburne reported: "Musketry and artillery at short range swept the open spaces between the tents, with an iron storm that threatened certain destruction for every living thing that would dare to cross."

That blast blew both regiments back down the hill. The 23rd Tennessee broke and kept running; Cleburne managed to rally about half of the regiment's survivors 100 yards back, but the others vanished. The 6th Mississippi reformed its battle line just below the tents and charged again.

Through the tents and up the hill they

At dawn on the 6th of April, 1862, Confederates spill out of the thickets around Shiloh Church in a surprise attack on General Prentiss' camp. The startled Federal soldiers retreated beyond their tents. But they soon formed a battle line that slowed down the Confederate onslaught.

came, the men almost running, yelping that shrill Rebel yell that put fire in their hearts. The Federal cannon roared and puffs of smoke flared from the 53rd's line. Flying metal slashed the Confederates. William C. Thompson of Simpson County, Mississippi, was in the charge. He ran along, noticing men on the ground, realizing that he could not see their faces and then thinking that he did not want to see them. Then he recognized his cousin, blinded by a shot in the face. There was a friend, dead, and another friend wounded. The cannon flashing again, violent pain struck Thompson and he went down. He heard his cousin calling; he tried to crawl toward him and fainted. He survived, but just barely.

The 6th Mississippi was destroyed. In a half hour it had lost 300 officers and men, 70 per cent of its strength. Only 60 men could form up to continue the battle with the reinforcements that arrived.

Even so, the Confederate charge routed the 53rd Ohio. At the height of the clash, Colonel Appler's strained nerve cracked. He bawled, "Retreat and save yourselves!" and ran for the rear with most of the men following. Adjutant Dawes, who was barely a year out of college, managed to hold two companies, but the rest fled.

Still, the hastily organized Federal line refused to collapse completely. Sherman on the right and Prentiss on the left managed to cling desperately to their ground, while behind them McClernand, Hurlbut and W.H.L. Wallace formed battle lines to stem the Rebel tide. By 8 a.m. it had become clear to the Confederates that Hardee's line was not breaking through as expected, and Bragg began to move up his corps, the second Confederate wave, to press the attack.

Grant was at breakfast in his headquarters at Savannah when he first heard the sound of distant cannon. He went onto the porch to listen. He was limping, having sprained his ankle when his horse fell in the mud the previous day. "Gentlemen," he said to his staff, "the ball is in motion. Let's be off." He made for his headquarters steamboat, the *Tigress*, which was standing by. As the vessel got up steam, he dispatched two brief notes calling for reinforcements.

One note went to Buell and the other to a division commander, Brigadier General William Nelson. Buell's army had begun arriving in Savannah, on the east bank of the river, the day before; Nelson's division was already there and the others were near. Johnston had failed in his crucial effort to destroy Grant's army before Buell's could link up with it.

Grant's note to Nelson ordered him to get a guide and move his troops to a point across the river from Pittsburg Landing. At Savannah, Nelson awaited river transport, but Grant had ordered none. This suggests that Grant still felt little urgency, since steamboats could have moved Nelson's men much more rapidly. In any case, Nelson's division had to begin by marching more than nine miles overland.

On the way to his main camp, Grant paused at Crump's Landing to tell Lew Wallace to get his men ready to move. Wallace had heard the cannon, and he told Grant that his men were ready now, but Grant had no further orders for him. At about 9 a.m., Grant got his horse ashore and began riding toward the front.

As Grant reached the battle, Prentiss' line was on the verge of collapse. A Confederate bayonet charge—sent in by General

The 11th Illinois fires by file at the advancing Confederates. But the defenders cracked after 10 minutes of fighting. "They fell back, I regret to add, without my order," wrote their commander, Colonel Thomas Ransom. He is seen on horseback in this watercolor by his brother Fred, a private in the regiment.

The Line of Battle

Fred E. Ransom, Artist

Johnston—swept across 300 yards of open ground and pushed Prentiss' men back to their camp. Everett Peabody, bleeding from four wounds, galloped among the tents, trying to rally the men for another stand. Then a musket ball went through his head, killing him instantly.

Prentiss' division held briefly in its camps, then broke and scattered. Private Leander Stillwell of the 61st Illinois saw something that sent a chill through him. "It was a gaudy sort of thing, with red bars," he later wrote. "It flashed over me in a second that that thing was a Rebel flag. It was going fast, with a jerky motion, which told me that the bearer was on the double quick." Stillwell suddenly wanted to get out of there, and he bolted for the rear.

It was too late for a boy of the 18th Missouri to escape. A chaplain found him screaming, with intestines protruding from an abdomen wound. The wound had contracted and was squeezing the bowel. "I feel as if my bowels are in boiling water," he cried. The chaplain reopened the wound with a penknife, pushed the intestine back in, told

the youth to trust in Christ and left him.

Fresh Federal units moving up encountered troops of Prentiss' routed regiments. These men were "rushing back from the front pell mell," one soldier recalled, "holding up their gory hands, shouting 'you'll catch it!—we are all cut to pieces—the Rebels are coming!'" The panicked troops clogged the road and infuriated the newcomers trying to advance. When a colonel rode up braying, "We're whipped, we're whipped; we're all cut to pieces!" a lieutenant in the 44th Indiana drew his pistol and threatened to kill the man. But nothing could stop the flight to Pittsburg Landing. The number of men in hiding at the river's edge grew all day, rising into the thousands.

Meanwhile Sherman's regiments were still giving ground, but still fighting stubbornly. Sherman, a handkerchief wrapped around his wounded hand, seemed to get calmer as the day progressed, even though four horses were killed under him. He remained boldly upright under fire that made his aides approach at a crouch; he watched the battle with narrow eyes, sending orders up and down his line, utterly absorbed. He was still standing there, an inspiration to his men, when Grant's aide-de-camp, Captain William R. Rowley, came up. Without looking away from his skirmishers, Sherman said, "Tell Grant if he has any men to spare I can use them; if not, I will do the best I can. We are holding them pretty well just now—pretty well—but it's as hot as hell."

Fleeing from the battle line, frightened Federal soldiers stream down to the Tennessee River to seek refuge under the bluff or swim to the other side. General Grant concluded that the thousands of fugitives would have preferred to be "shot where they lay, without resistance," rather than go back to the battle.

It was hot all along Sherman's line. Responding quickly to Sherman's appeal for help, McClernand advanced his brigade to plug the gap between Sherman and Prentiss. But the Confederate fire was withering. A ball pierced the hat worn by Private Thomas Haines of McClernand's 11th Iowa; he raised it aloft on his ramrod to show his comrades, and a shell exploded overhead, killing him.

General Hurlbut also dispatched a brigade to help Sherman. A young private in Hurlbut's 14th Illinois, suffering from a horrible stomach wound, came to his commander, crying, "Oh, Colonel, what shall I do?" A soldier in another of Hurlbut's units walked off the field with seven bullet holes in him,

General John A. McClernand wrote to President Lincoln after Shiloh, bragging about his risks and accomplishments in the battle: "My division, as usual, has borne or shared in bearing the brunt. I have lost in killed and wounded about every third man of my command. Within a radius of 200 yards of my headquarters some 150 dead bodies were left on the field."

and a friend said later, "He looked like he had been dipped in a barrel of blood."

In a ravine behind Sherman's line a Federal surgeon was working on wounded men who were being hit again where they lay. A soldier whose wounds were freshly dressed exclaimed, "This is a hell of a place for a hospital!" But there was no good place for a hospital. A wounded man who was sent out of Sherman's line to be treated found he was under fire from all directions and came back saying, "Captain, give me a gun, this damned fight ain't got any rear." Later, Sherman wrote his wife: "The scenes on this field would have cured anyone of war."

Finally, near 10 a.m., his left wing gone, both flanks being turned, Sherman gave the order to fall back. His stand had bought the Federal army a bit more time.

As Prentiss' front dissolved, the Confederates took a break. Some of the soldiers had not eaten in 24 hours and they stopped to wolf down the breakfasts left on the fires in Prentiss' camp and, in the manner of soldiers everywhere, to collect souvenirs. When Johnston rode into the camp, he spied one of his officers emerging from a tent with an armful of loot and said sharply, "None of that, sir; we are not here for plunder!" But, seeing the man's chagrin, Johnston softened. He picked up a small tin cup and said, "Let this be my share of the spoils today."

The interlude proved to be a blessing for Prentiss, for it gave him time to regroup. He managed to stop remnants of his command, perhaps 1,000 men, and align them on an old wagon road about a mile behind their original position. Sunken slightly from use, the road provided some cover; better still, it was on high ground, fringed with concealing brush and a stout split-rail fence, and much of it commanded a huge open field over which attacking troops would have to move fully exposed. Here Prentiss and his men decided to stand and fight.

At this point General Hurlbut aligned his two brigades (the third had gone to Sherman's aid) to Prentiss' left along the Sunken Road. And W.H.L. Wallace aligned his three fresh brigades on Prentiss' flanks, two on Prentiss' right and one far to the left beyond Hurlbut. This made Prentiss a crucial link that connected two divisions of fresh men along a strong natural position. To the right of Wallace's two brigades stood McClernand's division and then Sherman's. Thus at about 10:30 in the morning, the Federal line was formed again.

Grant rode forward to visit Sherman and found him worried; his division used ammunition of six different calibers and was running out of all kinds. Grant told him more ammunition was on its way and rode off. Grant's aide, Rowley, thought things looked "pretty squally," but Grant said, "Well, not so bad. Lew Wallace must be here soon."

Sidney Johnston was as imperturbable as Grant. When a Federal battery seemed to be getting his range, he coolly shifted position to a small ravine. He continually cheered his troops on, moving units up himself to plug holes, occasionally launching charges. At one point he encountered a terrified group of immigrant German prisoners from St. Louis; they clung to his stirrups and begged for mercy. "Why, men," he said genially, "you don't suppose we kill prisoners, do you? Go to the rear and you will be safe there."

When one of Beauregard's aides rode up to ask for any new orders, Johnston said: "Tell Beauregard that we are sweeping the field before us and I think we shall press them to the river." He had a few instructions, but he hedged them carefully: They were not orders and Beauregard was to act as he saw fit. Johnston seemed to recognize that he had waived control of the battle.

Beauregard had moved his headquarters up to Shiloh Church and was using Sherman's tent. Confederate soldiers remembered the fiery little man standing on a stump by the church, wearing his lucky red cap and urging them on. Beauregard had staff officers roving the battlefield and reporting back on where reinforcements were needed. His adjutant, Colonel Jordan, circulated about the field, giving orders in the name of Beauregard or Johnston. "I found the troops repeatedly halted for lack of orders," he wrote later. Usually, Jordan sent them off toward the heaviest firing, a military axiom much favored by Beauregard.

The three Confederate assault lines, which were now spread across the whole battlefield, were inextricably intermingled on the rough and broken ground of Shiloh. The crushing avalanche that Beauregard had envisioned was deteriorating in raging little fights. Men often were lost and some found themselves fighting in strange units under commanders they did not know. Generals lost touch with brigades, brigades with regiments and regiments with companies.

Finally Polk and Bragg met amid the confusion and decided to redivide the command. Bragg would take the right, Polk the center, Hardee the left, with Breckinridge in reserve. The two generals sent messengers to inform Hardee and Breckinridge.

Time was wasting for the Confederates.

These battle flags were carried at Shiloh by two hard-fighting Confederate outfits. Company A of New Orleans' Crescent Regiment *(top)* was among the units that accepted the surrender of Federal remnants surrounded in the Hornet's Nest. The 6th Arkansas Regiment attacked in the first wave and routed the Federals in their sector of the battle line.

The Federal line along the Sunken Road was growing stronger by the moment. At 9 a.m. Colonel John S. Marmaduke had tested it with a head-on assault by the 500 men of his 3rd Confederate States Infantry; Prentiss' troops responded with a blaze of musketry. The Confederates faltered, stopped in the wide field and turned back. This small success had the effect of stabilizing the Union line further.

Johnston now got ready to launch a mass attack with two strong, fresh brigades. But just then he was diverted by a garbled report that an enemy division was poised to strike the Confederate right flank. Actually, this was not a division at all. It was only a brigade—the one under Colonel David Stuart that had been fighting all morning to hold the extreme left—and with just three regiments it was understrength. Nevertheless this apparent threat prompted Johnston to divert the two fresh brigades that were preparing to assault Prentiss. He also ordered up part of Breckinridge's reserve and sent those troops along toward Stuart's position. The result was a delay of about an hour—a breathing space that Prentiss, Hurlbut and W.H.L. Wallace put to good use.

During the lull in infantry action, both sides brought up artillery and blasted each other's battle line. The Confederates soon got the range of the Sunken Road and laid a devastating fire on the men waiting there. Many of the fresh Federal troops were foolishly standing erect behind the rail fence; the scything metal fragments cut some of them down and taught the rest to lie down. John T. Bell, a 2nd Iowa private, later re-created his experience under the barrage: "I am lying so close to Captain Bob Littler that I could touch him by putting out my hand when a shell bursts directly in our front and a jagged piece of iron tears his arm so nearly off that it hangs by a slender bit of flesh and muscle." He said that Littler jumped up, cried, "Here, boys! Here!" and fell insensible. So terrible was the noise, said the same soldier, that "a rabbit trembling with fear rushes out of the brush and snuggles up close to a soldier."

The cannon fire drew the attention of Colonel Jordan, who was still carrying out Beauregard's order to find troops to send into battle. He saw a brigade from Polk's corps that had come up from the rear. Without further thought and with no semblance of a plan, Jordan told the commander, Major General Benjamin F. Cheatham, to launch an attack across the open field in front of the Sunken Road. The brigade was small— it had only three regiments—and at the moment it was almost alone on the field. Cheatham spied a body of men moving up behind him and assumed it would follow and support him. So he got his men ready. The new unit, however, had no such orders and it simply drew up and watched.

Alone in that great field that lay before the Federal position, the brigade formed two long lines and started across. They came on at a trot, closing the distance to the enemy 300 yards, 250, 200.

Colonel William T. Shaw of the 14th Iowa, in W.H.L. Wallace's division, moved his men onto the Sunken Road. He told them to lie down so they could see under the split-rail fence and ordered them to hold their fire. As the Confederates reached 150 yards' range, the Federal cannon opened up, raking them with canister in a cross fire, right and left. The long lines rippled like tall grass in the wind as the shot cut through. But those

still on their feet came on, running faster.

When the Confederates came within 30 paces of the fence, Shaw told his riflemen to fire. The 12th and 14th Iowa, he reported, "opened directly in their faces and the enemy's first line was completely destroyed. Our fire was only returned by a few, nearly all who were not killed or wounded by it fleeing in every direction."

On the extreme right of Cheatham's line, beyond the terrible open field, the Confederates came crashing through woods and brush toward Brigadier General Jacob G. Lauman's brigade of Hurlbut's division. Lau-

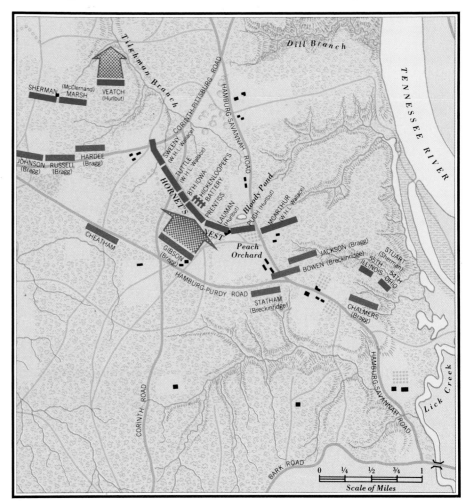

Around 12:30 p.m., Colonel Randall Gibson's brigade launched the first of a series of charges against the so-called Hornet's Nest, a Federal defense line centered on remnants of Prentiss' division and bolstered by units belonging to W.H.L. Wallace and Hurlbut. Later, on the Federal left, the brigades of Brigadier General John A. McArthur and Colonel David Stuart fell back in the face of an overwhelming attack by forces commanded by Generals James R. Chalmers and John S. Bowen.

Brigadier General Benjamin Prentiss rallied several regiments of his broken division to form the nucleus of the Hornet's Nest. Prentiss served with great valor, though his leadership was questionable. He rushed about, said one officer, "clamoring for he knew not what."

Colonel Randall Lee Gibson, following orders from General Bragg to attack the Hornet's Nest, led four charges that decimated his regiment. Gibson was accused of cowardice but his honor was upheld; in 1864, when he was 31 years old, he was promoted to the rank of general.

man had his men hold their fire until he could see the Confederate bayonets flashing in the brush approximately 100 yards away. Then he gave the order. The whole line erupted with fire, but the Confederates came on undaunted.

They came within 10 yards of the 31st Indiana before the Federal fire finally stopped them. Lauman said later that it made him ill when he walked out afterward and saw the battleground. The bodies lay in piles, some disemboweled, headless, cut in half by cannon fire. Everywhere wounded men cried and whimpered.

Stumbling out of that hell, a Confederate soldier gasped, "It's a hornet's nest in there." The name stuck.

General Braxton Bragg, now commanding the Confederate right, was determined to crush the resistance in the Hornet's Nest.

But for all his harsh, authoritarian manner, he was quite uncertain about how to do the job. And that, according to his colleague General Simon Bolivar Buckner, showed Bragg at his dangerous worst: "When he has formed his own opinion of what he proposed to do, no advice of all his officers put together can shake him; but when he meets the unexpected, it overwhelms him because he has not been able to foresee, and then he will lean upon the advice of a drummer boy."

Since the Federal line seemed impregnable to frontal attacks, Bragg might well have recognized the need to coordinate artillery with infantry to probe for weak points in the enemy line. Instead, he rode up to Colonel Randall Lee Gibson's fresh brigade and demanded a bayonet charge. Gibson, a young Yale-educated lawyer from a wealthy Louisiana family, had been awaiting orders. Bragg, however, took his rearward position as a

Captain Andrew Hickenlooper, mounted on his horse, Gray Eagle, directs his famous 5th Ohio Battery in the Hornet's Nest, a defensive position the Federals held through most of the first day's fighting at Shiloh. Hickenlooper's gun crews, though shorthanded, managed to fire withering blasts every 30 seconds.

sign of cowardice and that seems to have colored what followed.

Gibson immediately gave the signal, and the men of the 4th, 13th and 19th Louisiana and the 1st Arkansas started forward. Gibson's men had not seen the previous attacks, so they marched unwittingly across the open field toward the split-rail fence. Beyond it they could see brush but no enemy. The brigade found itself in almost impenetrable scrub oak at the edge of the field.

Then, from under the fence and through the scrub oak, a rain of bullets and cannon fire opened on them at point-blank range. The 8th Iowa's 800 rifles blazed at once, and Federal cannon, sited to slash the attacker's flanks, cut swaths with canister and case shot—explosive shells filled with iron balls. The fire seemed to come from so many directions that Colonel James F. Fagan of the 1st Arkansas was sure that he was taking fire from fellow Confederates as well as Yankees. Colonel Benjamin L. Hodge of the 19th Louisiana saw his men firing blindly into the brush and realized that they could see no more of the enemy than his muzzle flashes. Under this iron avalanche, Gibson's men went reeling back in confusion. The 19th Louisiana lost almost a sixth of its men in the charge, and bodies were strewn across the field.

Bragg's rage mounted at this reverse. He blamed Gibson entirely, charging him with "want of proper handling," and later wrote his wife, *"Entre nous, he is an arrant coward."* Gibson sent an aide to plead with Bragg for artillery support. But no artillery had come up behind Gibson, and Bragg's order was to charge again. The regimental commanders were furious. "I thought it impossible to force the enemy from this strong position

125

by a charge from the front," said Colonel Hodge, but he and the others set out immediately to try.

On the Federal side, Captain Andrew Hickenlooper, the commanding officer of the 5th Ohio Battery, positioned his 12-pounder brass James cannon in front of the Sunken Road and the 8th Iowa. At 1 p.m. the Confederates came running back across the field, yelling their Rebel yell. Hickenlooper fired canister until his guns were sizzling, but still the Confederate soldiers came on, and the Federal gunners and artillery horses fell at their posts.

The Confederate tide flowed and ebbed around the battery. "The enemy had captured the guns," said W. B. Bell of the 8th Iowa, "and taken them at least four or five rods when our men rushed forward and recaptured the guns and triumphantly sent them to the rear." That countercharge alone cost the 8th Iowa 100 casualties.

But Gibson's charge was broken again, and again his men reeled back over the bloody field toward their own lines. The ground was covered with dead and wounded from both sides. Then the undergrowth caught fire from flaming cannon-cartridge flannel, and the casualties screamed for a while until they burned to death. Artilleryman Hickenlooper found it "a most hideous and revolting sight."

Infuriated by the repulse, Bragg told his chief of engineers, Captain Samuel H. Lockett, to rally the brigade and carry its colors forward himself. "The flag must not go back again," Bragg said.

Lockett rushed to the brigade and seized the flag of the central regiment, the 4th Louisiana. Then Colonel Henry W. Allen of the 4th Louisiana loomed out of the battle smoke with bullet holes in both cheeks and blood dripping from his mouth.

"What are you doing with my colors, sir?"

On the left side of the Federal defense line, men of the 44th Indiana exchange volleys with Confederate attackers through a screen of dense smoke and flame. Brush fires on the Shiloh battlefield burned to death many of the wounded.

The peach orchard, devastated by fighting during the Battle of Shiloh, lies overgrown beyond the plowed field and rail fence in this postwar photograph. The picture may have been taken as a terrain study by artists preparing to paint the famous Shiloh cyclorama (*pages 130-135*).

Allen demanded. When Lockett explained, Allen snatched away his flag and cried, "If any man but my color-bearer carries these colors, I am the man." Allen also said that Bragg "must attack this position in flank. We can never carry it alone from the front."

But hardly had he spoken when Bragg galloped up and told Allen to advance. Appalled, Allen asked if they must charge again. "Colonel Allen, I want no faltering now," Bragg snapped.

In a rage, Allen started forward again. But his brigade was beaten back, and in a few minutes, on Bragg's new orders, Gibson again led what was left of his brigade over the same bloody ground with the same fruitless results.

By now it was 2:30 p.m. and the Confederate line had been stalled against the Hornet's Nest for more than two hours. Those four charges had shattered Gibson's brigade and ended with not an inch gained.

All along the line Confederate troops were being wasted in piecemeal attacks, usually without artillery support. No one bothered to mass troops for attacks along the whole line; when a Confederate regiment charged, Federal troops to either side were free to set up a brutal cross fire. Through the afternoon more than 17,000 Confederate troops were thrown against the Hornet's Nest, but never did more than 3,700 attack at once. Since anywhere from 4,000 to 5,000 Federal troops manned the position, the attackers actually were outnumbered by the defenders—a violation of the accepted doctrine that the force attacking a fixed position should have at least a 2-to-1 advantage over the defenders.

At the heart of the costly Confederate failure was the lack of an overall commander with a coherent strategy. Sidney Johnston and his corps commanders functioned as small-unit commanders. Beauregard, at the rear, contented himself with sending couriers about to order men toward the loudest firing. Some units spent more time marching than fighting as one order after another was countermanded by different generals.

While Gibson's brigade was being chewed up, Johnston's attention was focused on a peach orchard just to the right of the Hornet's Nest. The 10-acre orchard was in full bloom, a glory of pink petals that came showering down as flying metal slashed the trees. The rear of the orchard was on the Sunken Road, and Federal troops held a line toward its front. Johnston was determined to break that line.

Johnston ordered a charge into the peach orchard by a brigade of General Breckinridge's corps. But trouble soon developed. First a Tennessee regiment refused to fight, and then Breckinridge, sputtering with anger, reported that he could not get an entire brigade to obey his orders. "Then I will help you," Johnston replied. "We can get them to make the charge."

Johnston galloped over to the defiant soldiers and walked his horse, Fire-eater, slowly down their battle line. He held his hat in one hand and spoke to the men. "His voice was persuasive, encouraging and compelling," reported an aide, Governor Isham Harris of Tennessee. "It was inviting men to death, but they obeyed it." He touched their bayonets. " 'These will do the work,' he said. 'Men! They are stubborn; we must use the bayonet.' When he reached the center of the line, he turned. 'I will lead you!' he cried, and moved toward the enemy. The line was already thrilling and trem-

General Johnston lies dying on the field of Shiloh. "Johnston's death was a tremendous catastrophe," wrote one of his officers, who admired him to the point of idolatry. "The west perished with Albert Sidney Johnston and the Southern country followed."

bling and rushed, forward around him with a mighty shout . . ."

The wild charge sent the Federal troops tumbling back through the peach orchard to the safety of the Sunken Road. Johnston led at least part of the assault before he reined up. When Harris joined him afterward, Johnston's face was alight.

"Governor," Johnston cried, "they came very near to putting me *hors de combat* in that charge." He showed Harris his boot sole, which had been sliced off by a musket ball and was dangling from the toe. His uniform had been nicked in a couple of places, but he appeared unhurt.

In a moment Harris went off with a message, and when he returned shortly he found General Johnston reeling in his saddle. Harris grabbed him to keep him from falling and asked him if he was wounded. Johnston answered: "Yes, and I fear seriously." Frantically, Harris sent someone for help. Earlier Johnston had been accompanied by a personal physician, Dr. D. W. Yandell, but he had ordered the doctor to stay be-

hind to treat a group of wounded soldiers.

Harris guided Johnston's horse into a hollow and there lowered the general to the ground. Johnston had a leg wound that appeared minor, though his boot was full of blood. In fact, a Minié ball had nicked an artery in his right leg. It was not necessarily a fatal wound; had Dr. Yandell been there, he would have applied a tourniquet as a matter of course. Johnston even had a field tourniquet in his pocket, but no one on his staff understood how to use it.

Harris did not believe that the leg wound was the trouble—there must be another. But he found nothing. He opened a flask and poured some brandy into the general's mouth. An aide slid off his horse, knelt by his commander and cried, "Johnston, don't you know me? Do you know me?"

Johnston appeared to smile faintly and made no other sign. Soon he was dead. Now the Confederate army would have to make do with a leader, Beauregard, who was so far to the rear that he had only a vague idea of what was going on at the front.

The Hornet's Nest Reconstructed

Starting at 11:30 a.m. on April 6, 1862, about 5,000 Federal troops held a position known as the Hornet's Nest against a series of Confederate infantry charges. In the next six hours the defenders were gradually whittled down and eventually overwhelmed, yet their heroic stand gave General Ulysses S. Grant time to form a strong new defense line and to mount a counterattack, ensuring a Federal victory in the bloody two-day Battle of Shiloh.

This crucial struggle inspired the colossal oil painting shown on these pages in historic photographs. The canvas, 50 feet high and nearly 400 feet long, was painted 20 years after the Civil War by French artist

Concealed in the brush behind a sunken road, Colonel James M. Tuttle's Iowa brigade holds its ground against a Confederate attack on the Hornet's Nest at 3 p.m. Tuttle's line was bolstered by two guns from a battery of Missouri artillery (*background*) and four rifled cannon from the 1st Minnesota Light Battery (*foreground*).

Colonel Tuttle, accompanied by a mounted orderly, looks on as Colonel William T. Shaw (*on horseback, with drawn saber*) supervises the smoke-wreathed battle line of his 14th Iowa Infantry. Although the troops' view of the Confederate attackers was obscured by heavy foliage, a Federal officer wrote that "the groans and shrieks in the bushes told of the destructiveness of our fire."

Brigadier General Benjamin M. Prentiss, accompanied by two aides, exhorts the 8th Iowa to fight "to the last." With about 1,000 survivors of his shattered 5,000-man division, Prentiss held the center of the Hornet's Nest line. He was ordered by General Grant to "maintain that position at all hazards."

On the Federals' left flank in the Hornet's Nest, two companies of the 8th Iowa rush to the defense of Captain Andrew J. Hickenlooper's battery of Ohio Light Artillery. Hickenlooper, seen riding his white horse, described the Iowans' volley on the charging Confederates as "a sheet of flame and leaden hail that elicited curses, shrieks, groans and shouts, all blended into an appalling cry."

An Incomplete Victory

"No blaze of glory that flashes around the magnificent triumphs of war can ever atone for the unwritten and unutterable horrors of the scene of carnage."

BRIGADIER GENERAL JAMES A. GARFIELD, 20TH BRIGADE, 6TH DIVISION, ARMY OF THE OHIO; LATER U.S. PRESIDENT

General Beauregard wasted no time mourning Sidney Johnston's death. He immediately assumed command of the army and ordered that Johnston's body be shrouded for secrecy and that the bad news be suppressed lest it demoralize the troops. Then he made the mistake of turning his full attention to the troublesome Hornet's Nest.

On both sides of the Hornet's Nest, the Federal line was sagging back toward the Tennessee River. Beauregard might have hurled the bulk of his forces against those crumbling flanks and driven on to Pittsburg Landing, meanwhile containing the Hornet's Nest for later reduction. Instead, like Bragg before him, Beauregard seemed to be obsessed by the idea of smashing the Federal center.

Brigadier General Daniel Ruggles, the white-bearded commander of Bragg's first division, had seen how the Hornet's Nest consumed men. There had been 11 or perhaps 12 full-scale charges against this position, all of them bloody and unavailing. Clearly a new tactic was indicated. Ruggles began calling in cannon. Within an hour he had massed 62 guns in an irregular line facing the Sunken Road, where General Prentiss and his Federals lay. This concentration of artillery, larger than any yet assembled in an American war, opened up at about 4 p.m. and began hurling two or three rounds a minute into the Federal line.

To a 2nd Iowa lieutenant, that bombardment was like "a mighty hurricane sweeping everything before it." He saw men and horses flattened and dying all around him. Soldiers hugged the earth to escape the scything projectiles that screamed over them at waist height. In moments of silence between shellbursts, several miserable men heard the eerie sound of birds singing in the trees above them.

The cannonading went on for at least half an hour. It seemed like forever to the Federals, and they welcomed the start of a new Confederate infantry charge because it signaled the end of the bombardment. But now they faced the enemy alone; under the Confederate cannon fire, the troops on Prentiss' flank had begun to pull back, taking their guns with them.

The Federals' situation was even worse elsewhere on the field. On their right, Sherman and McClernand were fighting a desperate withdrawal toward Pittsburg Landing. And on their left, there were no troops at all; the Confederate forces had a clear path all the way to the Tennessee River and the vulnerable Federal rear. There Sidney Johnston's plan of attack came within an ace of succeeding, though more by accident than by design.

General John Breckinridge, whose reserve corps had taken the peach orchard while Johnston lay dying, joined an attack on his extreme right against Colonel David Stuart's isolated and understrength brigade. By mid-afternoon Stuart's men were perilously short of ammunition. They used up all the cartridges they could strip from the dead and wounded and then had to fall back. They plunged into a steep gorge 100 feet deep, and on the bottom they were caught in a cross fire from the mouth of the gorge and the cliff.

In the words of a Mississippi major, "It was like shooting into a flock of sheep. I never saw such cruel work during the war." To Lieutenant Lucien Crooker of the 55th Illinois, the gorge was "a valley of death." Crooker had been wounded three times and was being half-dragged, half-carried toward cover by Sergeant Parker Bagley when a bullet burned across Crooker's back and smashed into Bagley's side, killing him.

Stuart led his men out of the cross fire in the gorge; they would soon form a new line around Pittsburg Landing. His two regiments were ruined. The 55th Illinois had lost more than half its 512 men, and those still on their feet had an average of only two cartridges each. Wounded himself, Stuart left the field to seek medical help. The Federal left lay wide open for the Confederate drive that Sidney Johnston had envisioned.

But that drive did not come. The Confederates, exhausted and disorganized, took time to regroup. Then they moved to the left, toward the Hornet's Nest, where the sound of firing was heaviest.

The end was approaching for the defenders in the Hornet's Nest. The Federal withdrawals on their left and right had exposed their flanks, and Confederate infantry charges had hammered their flanks backward until their battle line had the shape of a horseshoe. With Confederate attacks coming now from both sides as well as the front, regiments in the Hornet's Nest were breaking up and pulling out of the open end of the horseshoe.

On the left in the Hornet's Nest, the 15th Michigan began to give way. George W. McBride, a youth with the 15th, remembered the terrible fear of being trapped: "Someone calls out, 'Everybody for himself!' The line breaks, I go with the others with the howling, rushing mass of the enemy pressing in close pursuit. The artillery seemed to have a crossfire and at short range was sweeping the ground with canister. The musketry fire was awful; the striking of the balls on the Sibley tents gave out a short, cutting sound that terrified me." Men were falling all around McBride, and he was driven by a mad thought: "I felt sure that a cannon ball was close behind me, giving chase as I started for the river. I was never so frightened before, never ran so fast, was never in such a storm of bullets. Out of that fire I came alive and unharmed, but it was a marvel."

Farther to the right, Colonel James C. Veatch's brigade was breaking up. Major John W. Foster, commander of the brigade's 25th Indiana, wrote: "Our left gave way and came sweeping by us in utter and total confusion—cavalry, ambulances, artillery and thousands of infantry, all in one mass, while the enemy were following closely in pursuit, at the same time throwing grape, canister and shells thick and fast among them. It appeared that all was lost." But Foster held his regiment out of this panicky mob until it passed. Then he coolly placed his men at the rear of the retreat and withdrew, fighting in good order.

In the Hornet's Nest, General W.H.L. Wallace ordered the outflanked survivors of his division to retreat before they were surrounded. While Wallace was withdrawing down a road, his brother-in-law, Lieutenant

Cyrus Dickey, spied enemy troops in the woods near the road and shouted a warning to Wallace. As the general rose in his stirrups for a better view, a ball struck him behind his left ear and emerged from his left eye socket. He groaned and fell to the ground on his face. Thinking that Wallace was dead, Dickey and several other men began carrying him to cover. But they dropped him and fled as more Confederate troops appeared. Dickey, now alone, dragged Wallace out of the road and then he, too, fled just ahead of the Confederates.

Colonel J. M. Tuttle, commander of the first brigade of W.H.L. Wallace's division, took charge of the withdrawal. Soon he found his way blocked; Confederate troops had completely surrounded the Hornet's Nest. "I ordered a charge and drove the enemy before us," he reported. Two of Wallace's four Iowa regiments broke through, but then the Confederate ring closed on the remaining two. Tuttle heard heavy firing behind him and determined to go back and rescue the trapped regiments. But it was too late; the firing ended and he realized that the other Iowans had surrendered. Tuttle then formed a new line to block the Confederate advance.

By now General Prentiss' force had dwindled to 2,200 men. The general had done exactly what Grant had told him to do that morning when Prentiss first took his position on the Sunken Road; he had held his ground at all costs through a dozen charges and scourging artillery bombardment. He had stood fast while Sherman and McClernand, Hurlbut and Stuart had given way and fallen back. He had held all through the long afternoon and in the process had delayed the Confederate advance while Grant and Hurlbut

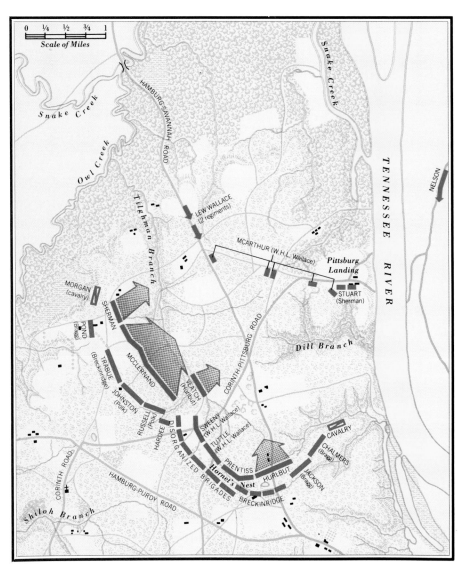

put together the new line that was forming at Pittsburg Landing.

Prentiss could do no more; he raised a white flag. And yet even then, men in his ranks refused to surrender. When a soldier in the 58th Illinois waved a white flag, his colonel slashed it down with his saber. A mounted Federal officer was told to surrender by a Confederate who had grabbed his horse's bridle; instead the officer fired and missed—just as a stray Confederate

In the afternoon, Generals Sherman and McClernand retreated to Pittsburg Landing, exposing units of W.H.L. Wallace's on the right flank of the Hornet's Nest. The left flank crumbled as General Hurlbut was driven back by the attacks of Generals Bragg and Breckinridge. By 5:30 p.m., the Hornet's Nest was surrounded and forced to surrender.

Confederate General Daniel Ruggles, whose massed cannon helped break up the Hornet's Nest at Shiloh, was a West Pointer whose men considered him cold, aloof and excessively severe. But no one faulted his courage: He had been twice brevetted for gallantry in the Mexican War.

ball struck him dead. Some Federals began smashing their rifles against trees to deny them to the enemy, and infuriated Confederates shot them down.

Colonel William T. Shaw knew exactly when the battle ended for his 14th Iowa. He had cracked his head on a low branch while trying to lead his men to safety through a thicket, and when he recovered his senses a 9th Mississippi major was standing before him. "I think you will have to surrender," the major remarked mildly. Shaw looked at his watch and it said 5:45.

Soon afterward it ended for the gallant 8th Iowa, which had withstood the worst of the Confederate attacks. The Iowans' commander, Colonel James Geddes, reported later to the Governor of Iowa: "Myself and the major portion of my command were captured at six o'clock p.m. and I claim the honor for my regiment of being the last to leave the advanced line of our army on the battlefield of Shiloh, on Sunday, April 6."

Through the long, dismal afternoon, while the defenders of the Hornet's Nest held the Confederate army at bay, the rest of Grant's army was falling back on Pittsburg Landing. Some of the units withdrew slowly and in order, defending themselves stubbornly and making the Confederates pay for pressing them. Some of Grant's units crumpled, broke and retreated in incoherent streams, although Grant was able to report, "With the single exception of a few minutes after the capture of Prentiss, a continuous and unbroken line was maintained all day." Grant organized a straggler net in an effort to stop the fugitives and assign them to regiments that were still intact. With all the units he could muster, Grant slowly built a new defense line.

The line ran inland at a right angle from the river above Pittsburg Landing northwestward toward Owl Creek. It was about three miles long and very strong. Grant's adjutant, Colonel J. D. Webster, a veteran engineer and artilleryman, rounded up all the cannon he could find and grouped them at the left of the line, where the weight of the Confederate attack was expected. On the right of the line, Grant posted the remnants of Sherman's and McClernand's divisions to protect a road that ran northward parallel to the Tennessee River. It was essential to keep that road open; Lew Wallace was expected to come marching down it with his division of 6,000 men, fresh and ready to save the day.

Grant waited for hours with mounting impatience and concern. Wallace was delayed

A Confederate cannonball decapitates a Federal officer during a staff conference behind Grant's last line of defense at Shiloh. The cigar-smoking general, talking with officers close by at left, barely escaped unscathed.

by a mix-up over orders and a long march down the wrong road. It was not until 7 p.m. or thereabouts that Wallace's division finally marched onto the battlefield and took position at the far right of the new line.

By then the first of General Buell's units, Colonel Jacob Ammen's brigade, had arrived on a march by way of Nashville and Savannah, Tennessee. Ammen was sitting on his horse on the riverbank opposite Pittsburg Landing when he received urgent orders to bring his men across. This surprised him, since he could see thousands of soldiers on the other side of the river milling about under the 100-foot bluff.

Ammen soon found out that the men were half-crazed fugitives from the battle who had eluded Grant's straggler net. Grant had tried in vain to rally the runaways at the river's edge. Once he sent a cavalry regiment to saber-whip them back into action. But they scrambled to safety on the steep sides of

the bluff, beyond reach of the blades, and when the horsemen gave up and rode off, they descended to huddle under the bluff again. Other fugitives, including some officers, were swimming across river.

While Ammen and the division commander, Brigadier General William Nelson, were ferrying their troops across the river, they saw frightened men swimming toward them. The captain of Nelson's riverboat stopped to avoid hitting the men in the water. Nelson, a blustery 300-pound Kentuckian known as "Bull" to his men, angrily ordered the ship to plow on. The riverboat moved forward again. On the swimmers' upturned faces an infantry officer glimpsed "such looks of terror and confusion I never saw before and do not wish to see again."

General Nelson mounted his horse as the boat landed and jumped over the gunwale to the wharf. He rode right into the mob along the riverbank, swinging his sword and roaring, "Damn your souls, if you won't fight get out of the way of men who will!"

Ammen followed Nelson ashore and heard a chaplain exhorting the runaways, over and over again: "Rally, men, rally and we may yet be saved, rally, for God and your country's sake, rally." In exasperation, Ammen shouted at the chaplain, "Shut up, you goddamned old fool, or I'll break your head. Get out of the way!"

Other units followed Nelson's division up the winding trail to the top of the bluff, where they were assigned to positions in Grant's rebuilt defense line. The men of one outfit, a Kentucky brigade, passed General Sherman as they moved up. It happened that these Kentuckians knew Sherman well and had no love lost for him; they had suffered under his rigid discipline while he was in the throes of his nervous breakdown as commander at Louisville.

But this was a different Sherman now. He had been riding up and down his line, encouraging his men, risking his life as freely as they risked theirs, and when he greeted the Kentuckians his face was blackened with gunpowder, his hat brim had been ripped away by shrapnel and he wore a bloody bandage on his wounded hand. The Kentuckians raised their hats on their bayonets and gave the general a lusty cheer. It was the first public display of approval that Sherman had received in a year, and he was deeply touched.

By dusk, it was clear to every man on Grant's new defense line that reinforcements had arrived, and cheer after cheer resounded down the line. The exhausted soldiers, who expected a final crushing Confederate attack at any moment, saw their salvation in the arrival of Buell's men. Buell himself, who

had reached the field well ahead of his 35,000 troops, also considered himself Grant's savior that day. But Grant and Sherman were less than effusive in their gratitude: They believed—with good cause—that the tide was already turning in their favor. The Confederates were not pressing the attack, and the longer they waited, the stronger Grant's new line became.

The Confederates had slacked off for several reasons. After the Hornet's Nest collapsed, a number of their units spent an hour or so rounding up the prisoners and herding them to the rear. Then, said a Confederate staff officer, "the news of the capture spread; many soldiers and officers believed we had captured the bulk of the Federal army and hundreds left their positions and came to see the 'captured Yanks.' "

It was after 6 p.m. and Confederate soldiers had been fighting for nearly 12 hours on empty stomachs; indeed most of them had not eaten since early the day before. Now, finding themselves in the enemy's well-stocked camps, thousands settled down at cook fires or went rummaging through Federal tents. Most of all, the Confederates were exhausted. They felt they had won a resounding victory and now, at last, was the time to rest. The feverish excitement that had brought them this far evaporated and left them drained.

Sensing that victory might be slipping out of their grasp, the Confederate commanders roused their troops and prodded them to make a last drive to capture Pittsburg Landing in the hour or so of daylight that remained. Fresh troops at this juncture might have made all the difference for the Confederates—but Sidney Johnston had committed Breckinridge's reserve corps rather casu-

This uniform coat, worn at Shiloh by Confederate Lieutenant Jeremiah Manasco of the 22nd Alabama Infantry, tells of his terrible wound. A shot shattered his left arm, which was then amputated at the shoulder. Manasco died a month later.

Steaming back and forth on the Tennessee River, the Federal gunboats *Tyler* and *Lexington* blast away at Confederate positions on the Shiloh battlefield, while downstream at Pittsburg Landing (*background*) transports disgorge reinforcements for Grant's hard-pressed army.

ally well before noon. There were no fresh troops available.

Slowly the exhausted Confederate units flogged themselves back into the battle. On their left, Hardee's and Polk's troops pecked away at Sherman's and McClernand's remnants with almost no effect. On their right, close to the Tennessee, Bragg's men faced massed Federal cannon across Dill's Branch, a marshy tributary flooded with backwater from the river. Grant had considered this flank a danger point and concentrated most of his guns here. In addition, two Federal gunboats, the *Lexington* and the *Tyler*, were lobbing heavy shells far inland; most of the rounds went overhead, but the shattering explosions in the rear intimidated many of the Confederates.

Two weakened brigades commanded by Brigadier Generals James R. Chalmers and John K. Jackson were the only units that Bragg was able to muster. From a vantage point on the edge of the ravine overlooking Dill's Branch, these troops could see in the distance the great throng of Federal runaways at Pittsburg Landing and mistakenly thought that Grant's entire army was gathering to oppose them. Against this presumably dangerous horde of 10,000 to 15,000 Federals, Jackson's men could rely only on their bayonets; almost all of them were out of ammunition.

Bragg exhorted the two brigades to a last great effort: "One more charge, my men, and we shall capture them all!" The troops plunged into Dill's Branch, waded the cold water and clambered up the steep ravine on the far side. There the steady, accurate fire of the Federal artillery cut them to pieces. Jackson reported later that his men "could not be urged further without support. Sheltering themselves against the precipitous sides of the ravine, they remained under the fire for some time."

Then Bragg received an order to retire. Beauregard's aide galloped up to him and cried, "The general directs that the pursuit be stopped; the victory is sufficiently complete; it is needless to expose our men to the fire of the gunboats."

Bragg cried, "My God, was a victory ever sufficiently complete? Have you given the order to anyone else?" Then, learning that Polk's regiments already were withdrawing, he said with a sob, "My God, my God, it is too late."

Later it was said that the Confederates had been on the verge of total victory when the withdrawal order ruined their chances. Samuel H. Lockett, Bragg's chief engineer and now an acting colonel, wrote, "In a short time the troops all were falling back—and the victory was lost." In fact, the offensive had already ground to a halt before Beauregard ordered the withdrawal, and the Confederates stood no chance of cracking the compressed Federal line, which was powerfully reinforced by thousands upon thousands of Buell's fresh troops.

Darkness fell and a terrible night began. The Federal troops had left their wounded behind with their dead on the ground that they lost. Neither army had any organized system of litter-bearers or medical teams to seek out and treat wounded men. So most of the wounded lay there, alone and unable to move, burning with the awful thirst that follows gunshot trauma.

Young Wilbur F. Crummer, lying exhausted in Grant's battle line, could hear the shrieks and groans of the wounded. He said:

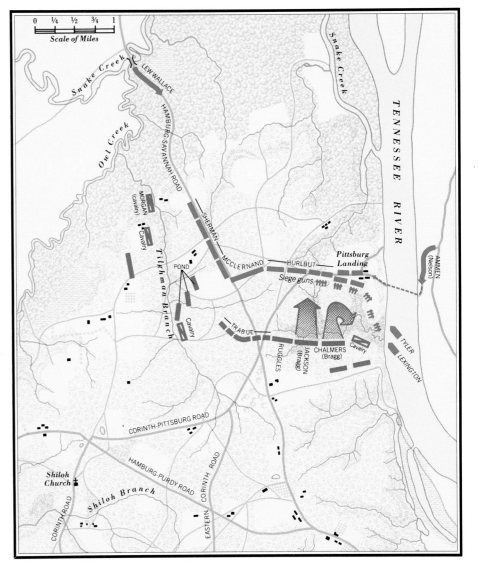

"Some cried for water, others for someone to come and help them. I can hear those poor fellows crying for water." And, Crummer added, "God heard them, for the heavens opened and the rain came."

But the deluge that night was no blessing. It began about 10 p.m. as a cold drizzle, and by midnight it was a downpour, whipped by a hard, cold wind from the north. Lightning flashes illuminated the ghastly field. "Sickening sights fell before my eyes," a young

In the evening, the Confederate attack stalled against a new defense line of routed remnants and fresh reinforcements under General Nelson of General Buell's army and General Lew Wallace. Massed Federal siege guns blunted a last charge by the brigades of Generals Chalmers and Jackson. At dawn, the armies of Grant and Buell launched an uncoordinated but decisive counterattack.

Mississippi private remembered later. "I saw a large piece of ground covered with dead heaped and piled upon each other. I shut my eyes." There were hogs out there gorging on the bodies.

Another Confederate wrote, "O it was too shocking, too horrible! God Grant that I may never be the partaker in such scenes again. When released from this I shall ever be an advocate of peace." One of Bragg's men said, "This night of horrors will haunt me to my grave."

The wounded suffered on and on. General W.H.L. Wallace lay in the rain, mercifully unconscious. Colonel Julius Raith, a brigade commander in McClernand's division, slumped against a tree, enduring in stony silence the pain of a shattered leg. An Iowa soldier hit above the eye had remained fully conscious but unable to speak, knowing that his comrades thought he was dead and were leaving him. He lay that way all through the rainy night and the next day. He was finally found on April 8.

Some of the wounded men summoned the strength to move. One hobbled into the line leaning on a broken artillery ramrod for a crutch. Many other wounded crawled close to one another for comfort or warmth. They died together and their huddled bodies were found the next morning. Three wounded youngsters, two Confederates and one

On a bluff near Pittsburg Landing, crewmen of Battery B of the 2nd Illinois Light Artillery stand at their five cannon for a picture taken a few days after the Battle of Shiloh. The 24-pounder siege guns, unusually heavy for a light artillery unit, still point southward in the direction of the Confederate attack.

Federal, crawled into a tent for shelter. They talked throughout the night, comforting one another. At dawn only one—a Confederate—was alive.

Scores of wounded men dragged themselves to a pond near the Sunken Road. They drank and bathed their faces. As more and more men came and collapsed by the pond, their blood turned the water red. The next day men saw the rusty color and named the place Bloody Pond.

Blood was everywhere on the field. When a Confederate officer's horse balked at dawn, the officer saw that rain had cut a ditch six inches wide down which "ran a band of blood nearly an inch thick, filling the channel." His horse "plunged his foot into the stream of blood and threw the already thickening mass in ropy folds up on the dead leaves on the bank."

All night long, the Federal gunboats on the Tennessee River kept hurling shells that landed among the wounded with earsplitting roars. All night the handfuls of surgeons on both sides were so desperately overtaxed they could treat only the most seriously wounded men. Shiloh Church became a Confederate hospital. Federal surgeons took over a log cabin that Grant had used as a headquarters and erected a few tents outside, but most of the wounded men who had been brought there lay in the rain awaiting treatment. The bone saws rasped all night, and by morning there was a pile of arms and legs outside the cabin. A drummer boy who fell asleep here awakened to find that he had been taken for a corpse and laid out neatly in a long row of dead men.

As the Federal transports came in with fresh troops, they were turned to use as hospital ships. The *City of Memphis* and other paddle-wheelers ran all day and all night carrying wounded men downstream to Savannah. There were so many wounded that most of them had to be laid down on the decks in the driving rain.

On one of the boats was Ann Wallace, the young wife of General W.H.L. Wallace. She had arrived unannounced that morning to visit her husband, but the battle erupted before she was able to find him. While she was waiting she began to treat the wounded as they came on board. That evening she received word that her husband had fallen. But God gave her strength, she said, to return to her wounded and to tend them there on her cabin floor, "lain close and in rows like bricks in a brickyard."

When Beauregard withdrew his troops that evening, he sent a wire to President Davis announcing A COMPLETE VICTORY. He later admitted: "I thought I had General Grant just where I wanted him and could finish him up in the morning." Most Confederate soldiers assumed that the battle was over; the Federals, they thought, would flee across the river in the dark rather than be driven into the river in the morning. Not one officer in 10, Bragg later said, bothered to replenish his unit's ammunition.

Beauregard's army was hopelessly scattered. Few units made any attempt to reform. And though some Confederate troops stayed close to the Federal line, Polk withdrew his division a full three miles. Bragg spent the night in Beauregard's tent instead of with his men. Beauregard ordered no reconnaissance of the enemy, perhaps because of an encouraging report that Buell's army had marched off in a different direction and hence could not be supporting Grant.

The report turned out to be entirely false.

The Confederates' prize captive, General Prentiss, discussed the battle freely and made a prediction no one believed. With a laugh, he boasted, "You gentlemen have had your way today but it will be very different tomorrow. You'll see! Buell will effect a junction with Grant tonight and we'll turn the tables on you tomorrow." Beauregard remained cocky. He slept that night in Sherman's bed.

Colonel Nathan Bedford Forrest, the Tennessee cavalryman, was not so confident. He dressed some of his troopers in captured Federal overcoats and sent them on a scouting mission behind the Federal lines. They reached the bluff overlooking the river and saw unit after unit of Buell's army crossing over. When Forrest got their reports, he raced to alert the command. He told General Chalmers that the Federals "are receiving reinforcements by the thousands, and if this army does not move and attack them between this and daylight, it will be whipped like hell before 10 o'clock tomorrow."

Next, Forrest awakened General Hardee, who told him to take the news to Beauregard. But Forrest could not find Beauregard and he returned frustrated to his camp. At 2 a.m. he scouted the river again and saw that Buell's soldiers were still pouring in to reinforce Grant's line. Again he awakened Hardee, who told him to keep a bright lookout. This casual dismissal made Forrest furious. Said an aide, "He was so mad he stunk."

Grant never lost confidence. Sherman found him that night with a cigar clamped in his mouth, his hat turned down against the rain, his coat collar up. Sherman thought of discussing the possibility of retreat but then changed his mind. "Well, Grant," he said, "we've had the devil's own day, haven't we?" And Grant replied, "Yes—lick 'em tomorrow, though."

Grant told Sherman he was going to counterattack at dawn. He said that the time would come, as it had at Fort Donelson, "when either side was ready to give way if the other showed a bold front." To a staff officer he added, "Beauregard will be mighty smart if he attacks before I do."

That night Grant elected to stay on the ground near his men, though he must have yearned for his warm, dry command steamboat, moored at Pittsburg Landing. "I made my headquarters under a tree a few hundred yards back from the river bank," Grant said. "My ankle was so much swollen from the fall of my horse that I could get no rest. Some time after midnight, growing restive under the storm and the continuous pain, I moved back to the log house under the bank. This had been taken as a hospital and all night wounded men were being brought in, their wounds dressed, a leg or an arm amputated as the case might require. The sight was more unendurable than encountering the enemy's fire and I returned to my tree in the rain."

As dawn broke, the Federal skirmishers moved forward all along the battle line, followed at a distance by the bulk of Buell's and Grant's armies. Neither of the commanders had laid out a firm plan of attack, and the phalanxes of troops advanced unevenly over the soggy ground. Soon the Federals crashed into an enemy unit—one of Bragg's—that had spent the night close by their front line. The Confederates, overwhelmed by the attack, fell back steadily, firing as they went.

General Grant's personal steamboat, the *Tigress*, lies moored between two troop transports at Pittsburg Landing a few weeks after the Battle of Shiloh. The *Tigress* had ferried Grant from his headquarters downstream at Savannah, Tennessee, to join the fighting on April 6.

Elsewhere on the battlefield, Confederate soldiers were jerked awake by the renewed firing and felt at once an awful sense of dismay. All of them were still exhausted, many were still hungry and few expected to have to fight again. Yet they climbed to their feet, found their weapons, hurriedly tried to round up ammunition and got ready to meet the onslaught.

Grant was moving 45,000 troops onto the field, half of them fresh. Beauregard could muster no more than 20,000 men capable of fighting, and all of them were weary and battered. The battle followed the odds, with Grant's men easily retaking most of the ground they had given up the day before. Yet even so, the Federals bumped into savage resistance around Shiloh Church. The Confederates there showed no inclination to give up more ground, and indeed they mounted assaults of their own on Grant's huge counterattack.

Time and again desperate Confederate charges smashed against the Federal front. Bragg ordered many of the attacks, resuming the tactics that had proved so costly the previous day. Brigadier General Patrick Cleburne, whose brigade in Hardee's corps had

Attacking under bursting shells, Federal troops led by Brigadier General Lovell H. Rousseau recapture and train on the enemy a gun battery (*foreground*) lost the previous day. They advanced in two solid lines against Confederates making a stand before Shiloh Church.

been decimated Sunday in the attack on Sherman, received orders from Bragg to throw what was left of his men against a Federal salient near the main road to Corinth. Cleburne protested that his flank would be left unprotected and his men destroyed, but Bragg refused to listen.

Leading the charge, Cleburne found himself in deadly terrain that he described as "a thick undergrowth which prevented my men from seeing any distance, yet offered them no protection from the storm of bullets. My men were dropping all around before the fire of an unseen foe." Cleburne's brigade had numbered 2,750 men on Sunday morning; scarcely 1,700 of them would survive Shiloh unharmed.

The sheer weight of Federal numbers kept crushing and grinding the enemy units. The Confederate brigade under Brigadier General Sterling A. M. Wood clung tenaciously to its ground not far from Shiloh Church, but a regiment on its immediate left was disintegrating, leaving Wood's flank exposed. Several times Wood left his brigade to rally the failing regiment; when he returned to his own command for the last time he found that all but two of his field officers were wounded. Then he saw that the regiment he had just rallied was collapsing again. Reluctantly he told his men to fall back.

In fact, the situation was hopeless everywhere for the Confederates. "The fire and animation had left our troops," one of Beauregard's staff officers wrote later. About 2:30 p.m., Colonel Jordan presented a painful proposition to Beauregard, carefully expressed in elaborate euphemisms: "General, do you not think our troops are very much in the condition of a lump of sugar, thoroughly soaked with water, but yet preserving its original shape, though ready to dissolve? Would it not be judicious to get away with what we have?"

"I intend to withdraw in a few minutes," Beauregard said. On his orders to round up remnants of broken commands to form a rear guard, Jordan collected 2,000-odd soldiers and a dozen artillery pieces and placed them on a ridge just south of Shiloh Church astride the road to Corinth.

Under this protection, the Confederate troops began to withdraw at about 3:30 p.m. They moved in orderly fashion, unit by unit, until Jordan's men were standing alone. Then they too filed off the ridge and down the muddy road in the train of the defeated army.

None of the Confederates retreated very far; in sheer exhaustion they began falling out after marching only a mile or two. Soon the entire Confederate army stopped and made camp. It might well have fallen easy prey to a vigorous Federal drive, but the Federals were also spent. Grant issued an order recalling his men, and they returned to the ruins of their original camps. Said Grant: "My force was too much fatigued to pursue. Night closed in cloudy and with heavy rain, making the roads impracticable for artillery by the next morning."

That morning, April 8, the battered Confederates set out for Corinth along a narrow road of deep, churned mud. Forrest was guarding the rear with 350 cavalrymen. In his wake came four brigades and a cavalry unit under General Sherman, who was less concerned with bothering the Confederates than with making certain that they cleared out of the area. When Sherman saw Forrest's cavalrymen ahead, he cautiously threw out skirmishers.

Watching from a rise, Forrest saw the Federal skirmishers pick their way through a belt of fallen trees, which gave the place its name, Fallen Timbers. The Federals were momentarily confused by the terrain, and Forrest chose that moment to strike. "Charge!" he bellowed. "Charge! Charge!" With sabers drawn and bugles blaring, the cavalrymen thundered down on the skirmishers, who fled back toward their ranks. The horsemen dashed among them, slashing right and left. Forrest raced on toward Sherman and his main force.

"I and the rest of my staff ingloriously fled pell mell through the mud," Sherman said later. He added: "I am sure that if Forrest had not emptied his pistols as he passed the skirmish line, my career would have ended right there."

Instead it was Forrest's life that almost ended. Leading the charge, he did not see

that his men had stopped at the sight of 2,000 leveled Federal rifles and that he was galloping forward alone. Not until he plunged into the Federal line did Forrest realize his plight. Then he whirled his horse and tried to cut his way out.

"Kill him! Kill him and his horse!" the soldiers screamed. A Federal jammed his musket into Forrest's side and fired. The heavy ball lifted Forrest in his saddle and lodged against his spine. Despite the wound, Forrest reached down, seized a Federal soldier by the collar, snatched him up onto the horse's rump as a shield and galloped away. As he neared his own men and safety, he flung the Federal to the ground.

Forrest was the last man wounded in the Battle of Shiloh.

The dazed Confederate survivors stumbled down the road to Corinth in a ragged column that stretched for seven miles or more. For the wounded, the journey was sheer agony. A civilian traveling with the army wrote of their ordeal: "Here was a long line of wagons loaded with wounded, piled in like bags of grain, groaning and cursing, while the mules plunged on in mud and water belly-deep, the water sometimes coming into the wagons. A cold, drizzling rain commenced about nightfall and soon came harder and faster, then turned to pitiless blinding hail. This storm raged with unrelenting violence for three hours. I passed wagon trains filled with wounded and dying soldiers without even a blanket to shield them from the driving sleet and hail, which fell in stones as large as partridge eggs, until it lay on the ground two inches deep."

The little town of Corinth turned into a charnel house. At least 5,000 wounded

A Wife's Ordeal at Shiloh

"The blow was too heavy to cause pain, suffering comes hours afterward." So wrote Ann Wallace of the news that her husband, Brigadier General William H. L. Wallace, had been critically wounded and left for dead in enemy territory on the Shiloh battlefield. She had arrived at Pittsburg Landing early on April 6 expecting to surprise him; instead she spent an endless night fighting her feelings of despair by tending the wounded.

The next day, Mrs. Wallace got another shock. Federal troops recovering lost ground found her husband wrapped in a blanket by some kindly Confederate; he was weak but still alive. His staff rushed him aboard a steamboat, where his wife joined him. "Will recognized my voice right off and clasped my hand. I had believed him dead! And he was alive! And he knows me!" Wallace was taken to Grant's headquarters at Savannah, and his wife kept a vigil at his bedside. "His pulse was strong and healthy," she wrote, "and we could not but hope that he would recover."

But his terrible head wound proved untreatable and became infected. On April 10 Wallace died. Said Mrs. Wallace: "He faded away like a fire going out."

The general was buried at home in Illinois. Then, to honor his memory, Ann Wallace arranged for the photograph shown below.

ANN WALLACE

Three mementos of General W.H.L. Wallace honor him in a haunting array at the door of his home in Ottawa, Illinois: his portrait in uniform, his horse and the flag for which he fell in the Shiloh battle.

men were laid out in homes and stores, on sidewalks and porches and railroad platforms. As news of the terrible casualties spread, women came from all over the area to serve as nurses. Doctors worked until they collapsed of exhaustion. Men languished for days with wounds untreated. Gangrene set in and the surgeons hurried to amputate. The pile of amputated limbs in the yard of the Tishomingo Hotel grew larger and larger. Eight out of 10 amputees died within a few days.

Infection spread fast among the wounded. Medicines were scarce and the precious supply of opiates dwindled. Sanitation was crude; the town's water supply was soon contaminated. Dysentery was universal, and typhoid was epidemic. Soon the sick list ran to 18,000 men.

Back on the Shiloh battlefield, identical scenes of horror lingered. For days, details went about the field collecting the wounded and digging mass graves for the dead. Many men reflected, as did Grant, that bodies lay so close together in places that one could have walked over them for great distances without touching the ground. The weather turned warm again and the stench of rotting flesh tainted the air.

Young Wilbur Crummer commanded one of the burial details. "When the grave was ready we placed the bodies therein, two deep," he wrote later. "All the monument reared to those brave men was a board upon which I cut with my pocket knife the words '125 rebels.' We buried our Union boys in a separate trench and on another board cut '35 Union.' "

The casualty totals were shocking and plunged the North and the South into grief and outrage. Each side lost roughly 1,700

Working hastily during the Shiloh battle, a Federal surgeon examines a soldier's wounded arm while other casualties await their turn for treatment. The tent facility, set up on the second day of fighting, was the first American hospital ever established on a battlefield.

A Federal Army sanitation crew burns the carcasses of horses killed in action near the peach orchard at Shiloh. In the battle's grisly aftermath, about 500 horses were found dead on the field.

men killed and more than 8,000 wounded. Far more revealing—and ominous for the Confederates—was the ratio of losses to the number of men who took the field. The much larger Federal army suffered only 21 per cent casualties of all kinds, while the Confederates, with a much smaller population to draw on for replacements, lost 27 per cent. It was no wonder that a Confederate soldier-novelist, George Washington Cable, later said, "The South never smiled again after Shiloh."

Who was responsible for these terrible losses? It was clear even on early judgment that the battle had been haphazardly planned and badly executed by both commands; the sole reputation to be greatly enhanced at Shiloh was that of the American volunteer as a courageous fighting man. Beauregard, who persistently called Shiloh a victory that nearly annihilated the Federal army, became an object of ridicule in the South. Grant was roundly criticized by the press and even by Congress for allowing his army to be caught ill prepared and to be attacked in a dangerously exposed position. The rumor that Grant had a drinking problem was revived. President Lincoln was urged to relieve Grant. But he replied, "I can't spare this man; he fights."

For all the blood shed at Shiloh, the battle was just an unexpected interruption in the Federals' campaign to capture the vital rail junction at Corinth. That piece of business remained to be finished, and the day after Shiloh, Grant's staff began pulling the army together to get on with the job.

That day, April 8, brought to a successful conclusion a separate but complementary Federal campaign that had been going on for nearly a month about 110 miles northwest of Shiloh. A joint offensive by Flag Officer Andrew Foote's river navy and 20,000 troops under Major General John Pope captured the key Mississippi River stronghold known as Island No. 10 (*pages 158-169*). This victory opened the way down the Mississippi toward Memphis, a major Confederate city connected to the rest of the South by a rail line running east through Corinth.

For the Federals' cross-country drive on Corinth, Major General Henry Halleck arrived at Pittsburg Landing on April 11 to take charge of the troops. Alarmed by the near-defeat, Halleck removed Grant from field command and appointed him to a new, meaningless post, second in command of the armies in the West. In fact, there was nothing for Grant to do. Humiliated, he thought about leaving the Army again.

One day Sherman paid him a visit and

The beaten Confederate army evacuates Corinth, Mississippi, as Federal forces under General Halleck advance on the town. When the victors entered Corinth, General Lew Wallace found "not a sick prisoner, not a rusty bayonet, not a bite of bacon—nothing but an empty town."

found him packing to leave. "I inquired where he was going," Sherman wrote, "and he said, 'St. Louis.' I then asked him if he had any business there, and he said, 'Not a bit.' I begged him to stay, illustrating his case by my own.

"Before the battle of Shiloh, I had been cast down by a mere newspaper assertion of 'crazy'; but that battle had given me new life, and now I was in high feather," Sherman continued. "I argued with him that, if he went away events would go right along, and he would be left out. Whereas, if he remained some happy accident might restore him to favor and his true place." Grant listened to his friend and stayed in the Army.

With his usual caution, Halleck refused to proceed to Corinth without making meticulous preparations. He reorganized the mauled Federal formations and called in fresh troops from the North. Not until he had more than 100,000 men and 200 guns did he launch his ponderous army on the 22-mile march to Corinth. Even then Halleck remained wary of a surprise attack. He advanced less than one mile a day and ordered his troops to erect elaborate breastworks each night.

There was no need for Halleck to be so careful. The Confederate army, battered and broken, was hardly in condition to fight. Although General Van Dorn's long-delayed army, now numbering 20,000 troops, had arrived in Corinth, Beauregard still could muster no more than half as many men as Halleck was leading.

The Federal troops finally arrived on the outskirts of Corinth on May 28, and the next day they began to bombard the Confederate defenses. Beauregard accepted the inevita-

bility of retreat, but in an effort to escape with his army intact, he mounted a clever deception. On his orders, locomotives chugged in and out of town periodically to the accompaniment of loud cheering. Beauregard's design was to convince the Federals that he was receiving massive reinforcements. The ploy worked. Halleck hesitated to advance until his troops heard the Confederate rear guard blowing up the supplies that could not be evacuated. When the Federals moved against Corinth on May 30, they occupied an empty town.

The loss of Corinth shook the Confederate high command. Jefferson Davis and his leading generals had considered the Memphis & Charleston Railroad the "vertebrae of the Confederacy"—and now Halleck had broken that backbone. From Corinth, the Federals could sweep eastward toward Decatur and Chattanooga, driving the Confederates out of eastern Tennessee, or move westward to Memphis. There, they could reestablish contact with Flag Officer Foote's Western Flotilla, which was steaming south from Island No. 10.

In the first year of fighting, the Confederates had lost Missouri, Kentucky and most of Tennessee. They had been defeated in Arkansas. They had seen, on April 25, a Federal fleet under Flag Officer David G. Farragut seize New Orleans and move up the Mississippi toward Vicksburg, the last major Confederate stronghold on that river. Beauregard did still have the army he had withdrawn from Corinth—a move that he proclaimed "equivalent to a brilliant victory." But unless the Confederates could launch a successful counteroffensive, the West would be lost.

157

The Battle for Island No. 10

As part of a general advance southward that led to the Battle of Shiloh, Federal forces in March of 1862 mounted a massive effort to capture a Confederate strongpoint blocking the S bend of the Mississippi River around New Madrid, Missouri. The objective was Island No. 10, so called because it was the 10th island south of the Ohio River's juncture with the Mississippi. The fortress—judged impregnable by many—had 19 guns and 7,000 troops, supported by five batteries on the Tennessee side of the river, as well as a floating battery and a flotilla of gunboats.

The Federal forces—the larger part of those that had recently seized New Ma-

Shielded by a peninsula jutting out from the Missouri shore, U.S. Navy ironclads and mortar boats exchange fire with Confederate batteries emplaced on Island

drid—were considerably more powerful, consisting of Flag Officer Andrew Foote's fleet of six ironclad gunboats and 11 mortar boats, along with 20,000 troops commanded by Major General John Pope. But Pope and Foote could not agree upon a plan of attack.

General Pope wanted to send his soldiers across the river below the island to cut off the defenders, with Foote's ironclads providing covering fire. But Foote considered it too perilous to allow his gunboats within range of the Confederate batteries. Instead, he started an ineffective artillery duel (*below*), described by an exasperated Army officer as "bombarding the state of Tennessee from long range."

In the weeks that followed, the Federals demonstrated ingenuity and courage, but to little effect. The issue remained at a deadlock until a Navy officer proposed a bold plan. Then, quite suddenly, Island No. 10 proved to be something less than impregnable.

No. 10. Beyond the two-mile-long island, U.S. Army batteries south of New Madrid (*top right*) engage enemy gunboats.

Digging a Waterway to Flank the Island

General Pope, tired of waiting for Foote to bombard Island No. 10 into submission, decided to bypass the stronghold. His plan was to hack a canal through the flooded fields north of the S bend in the Mississippi; his watery shortcut would take him to Wilson's Bayou, which emptied into the river at New Madrid (*map at right*).

For the starting point of the canal, engineers led by Colonel Josiah Bissell selected an inundated wagon trail between Islands No. 9 and 8. Bissell set 600 men to work with four shallow-draft stern-wheel steamboats and an assortment of tools, saws, lines and tackle.

While half the men cut and cleared, the other half followed behind, improvising the army's very own navy. They converted large coal barges into gunboats by mounting guns on makeshift platforms.

The first half mile, through a flooded cornfield, was easy. But then the trail ended in a forest of tall timber, and progress slowed to a crawl. It took eight days to cut a channel 50 feet wide to Wilson's Bayou two miles beyond. And then the men had to carve a passageway through an immense jungle of driftwood and fallen trees.

Finally, after nearly three weeks of exhausting toil, the canal was finished. But events would soon prove that its construction had been unnecessary.

MAP

SHOWING THE SYSTEM OF

REBEL FORTIFICATIONS

ON THE

MISSISSIPPI RIVER

AT

ISLAND Nº 10

AND

NEW MADRID

ALSO THE

OPERATIONS OF THE U.S. FORCES

UNDER

GENERAL JOHN POPE

AGAINST THESE POSITIONS.

Scale of Miles

Astride a raft, four Federals work a saw fitted to a rocker-like frame while a fifth guides the teeth into an underwater tree trunk. Saws often got pinched in the larger trees. One crew spent two and a half hours cutting a single stubborn stump.

160

Balancing on slippery logs, engineers break up a jam of driftwood in Wilson's Bayou. The current was so strong in places that the men were tied to life lines.

A Daring Raid in a Thunderstorm

At the end of March, while Pope's engineers were hacking out their channel, Captain Henry Walke of the *Carondelet* proposed a daring move by the Navy; he volunteered to steam past Island No. 10 and cut off its garrison. To improve Walke's chances of running the Confederate guns, Flag Officer Foote ordered a raid on the northernmost enemy position, Battery No. 1, a six-cannon outpost on the Tennessee shore about two miles above the island.

On the dark and stormy night of April 1, Colonel George Roberts of the 42nd Illinois Regiment and 50 hand-picked men left Foote's flotilla in barges. With muffled oars they rowed to shore. A sudden flash of lightning revealed them to two enemy sentries, but too late. The raiders quickly overran and overpowered the Confederates. The Federals spiked the Confederate guns and then returned to their fleet.

Boatloads of Federals swarm ashore near Battery No. 1 on April 1, 1862. The battery was one of five Confederate strong points outlying Island No. 10 on the Tennessee side of the Mississippi at Madrid Bend.

Running a Gantlet of Confederate Guns

Captain Walke spent several days preparing for the *Carondelet's* run past Island No. 10. For added protection, heavy planks were laid across the ironclad's deck, cordwood was stacked high around the boilers, and a hawser and a chain cable were wrapped around the pilothouse. A coal barge loaded with hay bales was lashed to the gunboat's port side, which would have to face the Confederate batteries. Now the *Carondelet*, an observer remarked, "resembled a farmer's wagon prepared for market."

On April 4, at 10 p.m., the *Carondelet* cast off during a furious thunderstorm. "Dark clouds rose rapidly and enveloped us in almost total darkness," recalled Walke, "except for welcome flashes of vivid lightning to show us the perilous way."

Running at full speed through the pelting rain, the *Carondelet* came abreast of Island No. 10. The Confederates spied her, but their guns, most of which were ranged along banks 20 or 30 feet high, could not be depressed far enough to hit the ironclad. Virtually untouched, the *Carondelet* raced past the island and past the Confederate floating battery, which managed to fire only half a dozen shots.

About midnight, the *Carondelet* docked at New Madrid to a jubilant reception from Federal troops. She had been hit just twice; a cannonball had dented the protective coal barge and another was found inside a bale of hay.

The *Carondelet* steams past Island No. 10 as Confederate artillery shells shriek harmlessly overhead. Flames spurting from the smokestacks had alerted the Confederate gunners.

Capping a Momentous Union Triumph

Once the *Carondelet* was safely past Island No. 10, General Pope's attack unfolded with clockwork precision. On April 6 the ironclad set out to clear the Tennessee shore of enemy batteries. In 25 minutes she destroyed two guns opposite Point Pleasant.

The next day, the *Carondelet* was joined by a second ironclad, the *Pittsburgh,* which had dashed past Island No. 10 during the night. Together they attacked Watson's Landing (*right*) and then provided covering fire for transports moving Pope's men across the river. By 9 p.m., most of the garrison at Island No. 10 had fled, and the rest surrendered.

The Confederate fugitives from the island headed toward Tiptonville, five miles to the south. But advance elements of General Pope's army beat them to the town and blocked the narrow isthmus between the Mississippi and Reelfoot Lake. In the early-morning hours of April 8, the last Confederate stragglers gave up.

It was a stunning victory for the Union. More than 5,000 Confederates, including three generals, had been taken prisoner. The anchor of the Confederate left flank in the West had been smashed—all with the loss of only a handful of Federals.

The *Carondelet* (*left*) and the *Pittsburgh* silence Confederate batteries at Watson's Landing, which guarded the escape route from Island No. 10. After a one-hour fight, the Confederate gun crews fled into the surrounding woods.

Victorious Federal troops draw up around disarmed Confederates during surrender ceremonies at Tiptonville, Tennessee, on April 8, 1862. In addition to the

prisoners, the Union forces had captured 7,000 small arms and vast quantities of ammunition and stores.

ACKNOWLEDGMENTS

The editors thank the following individuals and institutions for their help in the preparation of this volume: *Illinois:* Cairo—Louise Ogg, Cairo Public Library. Chicago—Teresa Krutz, Chicago Historical Society. Mounds—Guyla Moreland.
Maryland: Annapolis—James W. Cheevers, U.S. Naval Academy Museum.

Mississippi: Jackson—Roxanne Miller, Mississippi Department of Archives and History.
New York: New York—The New-York Historical Society.
Rhode Island: Providence—Mark H. Dunkelman.
Tennessee: Nashville—Marilyn Bell, Leslie Pritikin, Tennessee State Library and Archives; Gwen Billig, Photo Guild Lab, Inc.; Steve Cox, John Frase, James Kelly, Tennessee

State Museum; James Hoobler, Tennessee Historical Society; Bill LaFevor.
Wisconsin: Niles—Wayne Stiles, Fort St. Joseph Museum. Wisconsin Dells—O. W. Reese, H. W. Bennett Studio.

The index for this book was prepared by Nicholas J. Anthony.

PICTURE CREDITS

Credits from left to right are separated by semicolons, from top to bottom by dashes.

Cover: Courtesy the Seventh Regiment Fund, Inc., photographed by Al Freni. 2, 3: Map by Peter McGinn. 9: Museum of the Confederacy, photographed by Larry Sherer. 10, 11: Missouri Historical Society. 13: National Portrait Gallery, Smithsonian Institution, Washington, D.C. 14, 15: Courtesy Frank Wood. 16: The Thomas Gilcrease Institute of American History and Art, Tulsa, Oklahoma. 17: Library of Congress. 18, 19: Missouri Historical Society. 20: Library of Congress. 22, 23: Collections of the G.A.R. Memorial Hall Museum, Madison, Wisconsin. 24-26: Library of Congress. 27: State Historical Society of Wisconsin. 28: Prints Division, the New York Public Library, Astor, Lenox and Tilden Foundations—from *The American Soldier in the Civil War*, published by Stanley-Bradley Publishing Co., New York, © 1895, courtesy Library of Congress. 30, 31: Courtesy State Historical Society of Missouri. 32: Courtesy Frank Wood. 34, 35: The Western Reserve Historical Society. 36, 37: Cairo Public Library, Cairo, Illinois. 38, 39: The Western Reserve Historical Society; Cairo Public Library, Cairo, Illinois. 40, 41: Cairo Public Library, Cairo, Illinois. 43: Library of Congress. 44: From *A Personal History of Ulysses S. Grant* by Albert D. Richardson, American Publishing Company, Hartford, Connecticut, courtesy Library of Congress. 46: Illinois State Historical Library. 47: Cairo Public Library, Cairo, Illinois. 49: Fine Arts Gallery of the University of the South. 50, 51: United States Marine Corps Museum, photographed by Fil Hunter—National Rifle Association, photographed by Leon Dishman—courtesy Lee Carter, photographed by Fil Hunter. 53: From *The American Soldier in the Civil War*, published by Stanley-Bradley Publishing Co., New York, © 1895,

courtesy Library of Congress. 55: National Archives, Neg. No. 111-BH-1172. 56, 57: Kentucky Military History Museum. 58-61: Library of Congress. 62: Division of Naval History, National Museum of American History, Smithsonian Institution. 63: Library of Congress. 64: U.S. Naval Academy/Beverly R. Robinson Collection. 65: Kentucky Military History Museum. 66, 67: Courtesy Frank Wood. 68-71: U.S. Army Military History Institute, copied by Robert Walch. 72, 73: Kean Archives; courtesy Frank Wood—U.S. Army Military History Institute, copied by Robert Walch. 74, 75: National Archives, Neg. No. 165-C-702. 76, 77: Courtesy The New-York Historical Society. 80: Courtesy Richard P. W. Williams. 82, 83: Courtesy Frank Wood. 85: From *Battles and Leaders of the Civil War*, published by The Century Co., 1884. 86, 87: The Museum of the Confederacy; Library of Congress (2); Valentine Museum, Richmond, Virginia. 88, 89: Chicago Historical Society, Neg. No. 1920.1645. 92-94: Courtesy Frank Wood. 95: Courtesy of the Tennessee State Museum, photographed by Stephen D. Cox. 96, 97: From *The American Soldier in the Civil War*, published by Stanley-Bradley Publishing Co., New York, © 1895, courtesy Library of Congress—courtesy Frank Wood. 99: Mississippi State Historical Museum, a division of the Department of Archives and History. 100, 101: Library of Congress. 102, 103: Tennessee State Museum, photographed by Bill LaFevor. 105: City of Niles, Michigan/Fort St. Joseph Museum. 106: The State Historical Society of Missouri. 107: Tennessee Historical Society. 108, 109: Courtesy Byron J. Ihle; Florida Photographic Collection, Florida State Archives. 110: From *The Life of General Albert Sidney Johnston* by William Preston Johnston, published by D. Appleton and Co., New York, 1878. 112: Map by Walter Roberts. 113: Courtesy Christopher Nelson. 114: U.S. Army Military History Institute, copied by James Enos. 115:

The American Heritage Picture Collection. 117: Frederick E. Ransom Sketchbook, Illinois State Historical Library. 118: Courtesy Frank Wood. 119: Library of Congress. 121: Confederate Memorial Hall, photographed by Bill van Calsem—Old State House, Little Rock, Arkansas. 122: Map by Walter Roberts. 123: Library of Congress; Courtesy Herb Peck Jr. 124, 125: Courtesy the Cincinnati Historical Society. 126: Library of Congress. 127: Chicago Historical Society, Neg. No. ICHIi-08002. 129: Kentucky Military History Museum. 130-135: Henry H. Bennett. 138: Map by Walter Roberts. 139: Library of Congress. 140: From *A Personal History of Ulysses S. Grant* by Albert D. Richardson, American Publishing Co., Hartford, Connecticut, courtesy Library of Congress. 141: From the Collection of Philip Baron Ennis, courtesy Moss Publications. 142, 143: Courtesy of The Mariners' Museum, Newport News, Virginia. 144: Map by Walter Roberts. 145: Library of Congress. 146: Library of Congress—the American Heritage Picture Collection. 148, 149: U.S. Army Military History Institute, copied by James Enos. 150: Prints Division, the New York Public Library, Astor, Lenox and Tilden Foundations. 151: Library of Congress. 153: Illinois State Historical Library; Chicago Historical Society. 154, 155: From *Battles and Leaders of the Civil War*, published by The Century Co., New York, 1884—Library of Congress. 156, 157: From *Le Monde illustré*, Photo Musée de la Marine, Paris. 158, 159: Courtesy Frank Wood. 160: Courtesy Frank Wood—from *Battles and Leaders of the Civil War*, published by The Century Co., New York, 1884. 161-163: From *The American Soldier in the Civil War*, published by Stanley-Bradley Publishing Co., New York, © 1895, courtesy Library of Congress. 164, 165: Library of Congress. 166, 167: The American Heritage Picture Collection. 168, 169: Courtesy Frank Wood.

BIBLIOGRAPHY

BOOKS
Adamson, Hans Christian, *Rebellion in Missouri, 1861*. Chilton Company, 1961.
Ambrose, Stephen E., *Halleck: Lincoln's Chief of Staff*. Louisiana State University Press, 1962.
Anderson, Bern, *By Sea and by River: The Naval History of the Civil War*. Alfred A. Knopf, 1962.
Anderson, Galusha, *The Story of a Border City during the Civil War*. Little, Brown and Co., 1908.
Bearss, Edwin C., *The Fall of Fort Henry*. Eastern National Park and Monument Association, Dover, Tennessee. No date.

Bell, John T., *Tramps and Triumphs of the Second Iowa Infantry*. Gibson, Miller & Richardson, 1886.
Boatner, Mark Mayo, III, *The Civil War Dictionary*. David McKay Company, Inc., 1959.
Brinton, John Hill, *Personal Memoirs of John Hill Brinton, Major and Surgeon U.S.V., 1861-1865*. The Neale Publishing Company, 1914.
Castel, Albert, *General Sterling Price and the Civil War in the West*. Louisiana State University Press, 1968.
Catton, Bruce:
Grant Moves South. Little, Brown and Company, 1960.
Terrible Swift Sword (*The Centennial History of the Civil

War*, Vol. 2). Pocket Books, 1963.
This Hallowed Ground. Pocket Books, 1956.
Conger, Arthur Latham, *The Rise of U. S. Grant*. Books for Libraries Press, 1970.
Connelly, Thomas Lawrence, *Army of the Heartland: The Army of Tennessee, 1861-1865*. Louisiana State University Press, 1967.
Coons, John W., *Indiana at Shiloh: Report of the Commission*. Indiana Shiloh National Park Commission, 1904.
Crummer, Wilbur F., *With Grant at Fort Donelson, Shiloh and Vicksburg*. E. C. Crummer & Co., 1915.
Davis, William C.:

Breckinridge: Statesman, Soldier, Symbol. Louisiana State University Press, 1974.

Shadows of the Storm (The Image of War: 1861-1865, Vol. 1). Doubleday & Co., Inc., 1981.

Driggs, George W., *Opening of the Mississippi; or Two Years' Campaigning in the South-West.* Wm. J. Park & Co., 1864.

Duke, Basil W., *A History of Morgan's Cavalry.* Indiana University Press, 1960.

Egan, Ferol, *Frémont: Explorer for a Restless Nation.* Doubleday and Company, Inc., 1977.

Esposito, Vincent J., ed., *The West Point Atlas of American Wars,* Vol. 1. Frederick A. Praeger, Publishers, 1959.

Fiske, John, *The Mississippi Valley in the Civil War.* Houghton, Mifflin and Company, 1900.

Foote, Shelby, *The Civil War, a Narrative: Fort Sumter to Perryville.* Random House, 1958.

Force, M. F., *From Fort Henry to Corinth (Campaigns of the Civil War:* Vol. 2). Charles Scribner's Sons, 1881.

Fuller, J.F.C., *The Generalship of Ulysses S. Grant.* Kraus Reprint Co., 1977.

Gosnell, Harpur Allen, *Guns on the Western Waters: The Story of the River Gunboats in the Civil War.* Louisiana State University Press, 1949.

Grant, Ulysses S., *Personal Memoirs of U. S. Grant.* Ed. by E. B. Long. Da Capo Press, 1982.

Hammock, John C., ed., *With Honor Untarnished.* Pioneer Press, 1961.

Henry, Robert Selph, *"First with the Most" Forrest.* Bobbs-Merrill Company, 1944.

Hoppin, James Mason, *Life of Andrew Hull Foote, Rear-Admiral United States Navy.* Harper & Brothers, Publishers, 1874.

Horn, Stanley F., *The Army of Tennessee.* University of Oklahoma Press, 1953.

Hughes, Nathaniel Cheairs, Jr., *General William J. Hardee: Old Reliable.* Louisiana State University Press, 1965.

Johnson, Robert Underwood, and Clarence Clough Buel, eds., *Battles and Leaders of the Civil War,* Vol. 1. Thomas Yoseloff, Inc., 1956.

Johnston, William Preston, *The Life of Gen. Albert Sidney Johnston.* D. Appleton and Company, 1878.

Jones, Archer, *Confederate Strategy from Shiloh to Vicksburg.* Louisiana State University Press, 1961.

Lewis, Lloyd:
Captain Sam Grant. Little, Brown and Co., 1950.
Sherman: Fighting Prophet. Harcourt, Brace and Company, 1932.

Liddell Hart, B. H., *Sherman: Soldier, Realist, American.* Greenwood Press Publishers, 1978.

McDonough, James Lee, *Shiloh—in Hell before Night.* The University of Tennessee Press, 1977.

McElroy, John, *The Struggle for Missouri.* The National Tribune Co., 1909.

McFeely, William S., *Grant: A Biography.* W. W. Norton & Company, 1981.

McPherson, James M., *Ordeal By Fire: The Civil War and Reconstruction.* Alfred A. Knopf, 1982.

McWhiney, Grady, *Braxton Bragg and Confederate Defeat:* Vol. 1, *Field Command.* Columbia University Press, 1969.

Miller, Francis Trevelyan, ed., *Photographic History of the Civil War,* Vol. 1. The Review of Reviews Company, 1912.

Milligan, John D.:
From the Fresh-Water Navy: 1861-64. United States Naval Institute, 1970.
Gunboats down the Mississippi. Arno Press, 1980.

Monaghan, Jay, *Civil War on the Western Border: 1854-1865.* Little, Brown and Company, 1955.

Morrison, Marion, *A History of the Ninth Regiment Illinois Volunteer Infantry.* John S. Clark, Printer, 1864.

Nevin, David, and the Editors of Time-Life Books, *The Mexican War* (The Old West series). Time-Life Books, 1978.

Nevins, Allan:
Fremont: Pathmarker of the West. Frederick Ungar Publishing Co., 1961.
War Becomes Revolution, 1862-1863 (The War for the Union: Vol. 2). Charles Scribner's Sons, 1960.

Nichols, James L., *Confederate Engineers (Confederate Centennial Studies,* No. 5). Confederate Publishing Company, Inc., 1957.

Parks, Joseph Howard, *General Leonidas Polk C.S.A.: The Fighting Bishop.* Louisiana State University Press, 1962.

Parrish, William Earl, *Turbulent Partnership: Missouri and the Union, 1861-1865.* University of Missouri Press, 1963.

Polk, William M., *Leonidas Polk: Bishop and General.* Longmans, Green, and Co., 1915.

Randall, J. G., and David Donald, *The Divided Union.* Little, Brown and Company, 1961.

Rea, Ralph R., *Sterling Price: The Lee of the West.* Pioneer Press, 1959.

Rerick, John H., *The Forty-Fourth Indiana Volunteer Infantry.* Lagrange, Indiana, 1880.

Richardson, Albert D., *Personal History of Ulysses S. Grant.* American Publishing Company, 1868.

Roland, Charles P., *Albert Sidney Johnston: Soldier of Three Republics.* University of Texas Press, 1964.

Rombauer, Robert J., *The Union Cause in St. Louis in 1861: An Historical Sketch.* St. Louis Municipal Centennial Year, 1909.

Rood, Hosea W., *Story of the Service of Company E, and of the Twelfth Wisconsin Regiment of Veteran Volunteer Infantry, in the War of the Rebellion.* No date.

Smith, Edward Conrad, *The Borderland in the Civil War.* The Macmillan Company, 1927.

Smith, Page, *Trial by Fire.* McGraw-Hill Book Company, 1982.

Snead, Thomas L., *The Fight for Missouri.* Charles Scribner's Sons, 1886.

Stuart, Addison A., *Iowa Colonels and Regiments.* Mills & Company, 1865.

Sword, Wiley, *Shiloh: Bloody April.* William Morrow & Company, Inc., 1974.

United States General Staff School, *Source Book of Fort Henry and Fort Donelson Campaigns: February, 1862.* The General Service Schools Press, 1923.

United States Navy, *Dictionary of American Naval Fighting Ships,* Vols. 1-8. Navy Department, Office of the Chief of Naval Operations, 1977.

United States War Department: *Official Records of the Union and Confederate Navies in the War of the Rebellion,* Vol. 22. Government Printing Office, 1908.
The War of the Rebellion: A Compilation of the Official Records of the Union and Confederate Armies. Government Printing Office, 1902.

Walke, Henry, *Naval Scenes and Reminiscences of the Civil War in the United States on the Southern and Western Waters during the Years 1861, 1862 and 1863, with the History of That Period.* F. R. Reed & Company, 1877.

Wallace, Lew, *An Autobiography.* Harper & Brothers Publishers, 1906.

Wheeler, Richard, *We Knew William Tecumseh Sherman.* Thomas Y. Crowell Company, 1977.

Williams, Kenneth P., *Lincoln Finds a General: A Military Study of the Civil War.* The Macmillan Company, 1952.

Williams, T. Harry, *P.G.T. Beauregard: Napoleon in Gray.* Louisiana State University Press, 1955.

Wills, Charles W., *Army Life of an Illinois Soldier.* Ed. by Mary E. Kellogg. Globe Printing Company, 1906.

Wilson, James Harrison, *The Life of John A. Rawlins.* J. J. Little & Ives Co., 1916.

Wyeth, John Allan:
Life of General Nathan Bedford Forrest. Press of Morningside Bookshop, 1975.
That Devil Forrest: Life of General Nathan Bedford Forrest. Harper & Brothers Publishers, 1959.

OTHER SOURCES:

Bearss, Edwin C., and Howard P. Nash, "Fort Henry," *Civil War Times Illustrated,* November 1965.

Callender, Eliot, "What A Boy Saw On the Mississippi," *Military Essays and Recollections,* Vol. 1, Commandery of the State of Illinois, Military Order of the Loyal Legion of the United States, A. C. McClurg and Company, 1891.

Chitty, Arthur Ben, "A Mediocre General but a Great Bishop: Leonidas Polk," *Civil War Times Illustrated,* October 1963.

Eisenschiml, Otto, "The 55th Illinois at Shiloh," *Journal of the Illinois State Historical Society,* Vol. 56, 1963.

"First Reunion of Iowa's Hornet's Nest Brigade: 2d, 7th, 8th, 12th and 14th Infantry," Globe Printing Company, 1888.

Greenawalt, John G., "A Charge at Fort Donelson, February 15, 1862," Commandery of the District of Columbia, Military Order of the Loyal Legion of the United States, War Paper No. 41, 1902.

Harland, W. D., and T. C. Watkins, "Fort Donelson, Tennessee," Cairo Public Library Manuscript Collection, Cairo, Illinois, no date.

Harrison, Lowell H., "Mill Springs, 'The Brilliant Victory,'" *Civil War Times Illustrated,* January 1972.

Hickenlooper, Andrew, "The Battle of Shiloh," *Sketches of War History,* Vol. 5, Ohio Commandery, Military Order of the Loyal Legion of the United States, Robert Clarke Company, 1903.

Jordan, Thomas, "The Battle of Shiloh," *Southern Historical Society Papers,* Vol. 35, 1907.

Kurtz, Henry I., "The Battle of Belmont," *Civil War Times Illustrated,* June 1963.

McBride, George W., "My Recollections of Shiloh," *Blue and Gray: The Patriotic American Magazine,* January 1894.

Rector, John F., "Tells of Cairo 51 Years Ago," Cairo Public Library Manuscripts Collection, Cairo, Illinois, no date.

"Reunions of Taylor's Battery," The Craig Press, February 1890.

Roland, Charles P., "Albert Sidney Johnston and the Loss of Forts Henry and Donelson," *The Journal of Southern History,* February 1957.

Seaton, John, "The Battle of Belmont, November 7, 1861," Kansas Commandery of the Military Order of the Loyal Legion of the United States, War Paper No. 22, no date.

Stover, Frances, "The Panorama Painters' Days of Glory," Milwaukee County Historical Center, 1969.

Walker, Peter Franklin:
"Building a Tennessee Army," *Tennessee Historical Quarterly,* June 1957.
"Command Failure: The Fall of Forts Henry and Donelson," *Tennessee Historical Quarterly,* December 1957.

INDEX